2/15/03
Oreen ✓ S0-AQJ-832

Acts & Contrition

by Jim Moore

BAKER'S
PLAYS

100 Chauncy Street	*Western States*	*Canadian*
Boston MA 02111-1783	*Representative*	*Representative*
	Samuel French, Inc.	Samuel French, Ltd.
	7623 Sunset Blvd.	100 Lombard St., Lower Level
	Hollywood CA 90046	Toronto, M5C 1M3 Canada

NOTICE

This book is offered for sale at the price quoted only on the understanding that, if any additional copies of the whole or any part are necessary for its production, such additional copies will be purchased. The attention of all purchasers is directed to the following: This work is protected under the copyright laws of the United States of America, in the British Empire, including the Dominion of Canada, and all other countries adhering to the Universal Copyright Convention. Violations of the Copyright Law are punishable by fine or imprisonment, or both. The copying or duplication of this work or any part of this work, by hand or by any process, is an infringement of the copyright and will be vigorously prosecuted.

This play may not be produced by amateurs or professionals for public or private performance without first submitting application for performing rights. Royalties are due on all performances whether for charity or gain, or whether admission is charged or not. Since performance of this play without the payment of the royalty fee renders anybody participating liable to severe penalties imposed by the law, anybody acting in this play should be sure, before doing so, that the royalty fee has been paid. Professional rights, reading rights, radio broadcasting, television and all mechanical rights, etc. are strictly reserved. Application for performing rights should be made directly to BAKER'S PLAYS, 100 Chauncy Str., Boston, MA 02111.

Whenever the play is produced, the author's name must be carried in all publicity, advertising and programs. Also, the following notice must appear on all printed programs, 'Produced by special arrangement with Baker's Plays, Boston, MA.'

Amateur royalty (production fee) for ACTS & CONTRITION is $40.00 for each performance, subject to change, payable one week in advance of the production. Consult Baker Catalogue for current royalty information.

Copyright © 1997 by Jim Moore

ACTS & CONTRITION

Acts & Contrition was first presented on November 14, 1991 by the Celtic Theatre Company at the Seton Hall University Theatre-in-the-Round, South Orange, New Jersey, USA. The director was James P. McGlone. The set designer was Peter M. Reader. The lighting designer was Laurie J. Reader. The stage manager was Cindy Bitowf. The cast was as follows:

MSGR. FRANCIS RYAN .... Mark Fallon
MRS. HARRIGAN .... Jennifer Moore
TIPPLES NOLAN .... Glen Albright
FR. SEAN CONNALLY .... Joseph McGlone
KATY THOMPSON .... Barbara Marino
PEGGY KEENAN .... Eileen Fallon
BILLY THOMPSON .... Patrick A. Hughes
JOSEPH CONNALLY .... Mark Roger

*In loving memory
of Mary Jane Gilmartin*

CHARACTERS

MSGR. FRANCIS RYAN — A Roman Catholic priest, and pastor of Holy Contrition Roman Catholic Parish. A native of the parish, he is in his late 60's.

MRS. HARRIGAN — The rectory housekeeper, and parish busybody. She is in her late 70's.

TIPPLES NOLAN — The neighborhood drunk. He is a contemporary of Mrs. Harrigan.

FR. SEAN CONNALLY — A young priest in his late 20's, also a Contrition parish native. He began his vocation with fervor, only to see that fervor diminished by the mundane realities of everyday life in the suburban parish to which he was assigned.

KATY THOMPSON — A contemporary and old friend of Msgr. Ryan. A widow, she has been in poor health since the death of her husband several years ago.

PEGGY KEENAN — Katy Thompson's daughter. She is a contemporary of Fr. Sean Connally. She was also his high school girlfriend. The widow of a slain police officer, she now cares for her mother.

BILLY THOMPSON — Peggy's younger brother. He is a 20 year-old college student.

JOSEPH CONNALLY — Sean Connally's father, and a contemporary of Msgr. Ryan. A local tavern owner, he is estranged from his wife due to his taste for extramarital activities.

SCENE

The urban neighborhood served by Holy Contrition Roman Catholic Church.

TIME

The present.

ACTS & CONTRITION

ACT I, Scene 1

(*SETTING: We are in the parish office of Holy Contrition Roman Catholic Church, an urban parish in the Northeastern United States.*

AT RISE: It is mid-morning on a Saturday. Msgr. Francis Ryan is smoking a pipe and lining up a shot at a dart board.)

MSGR. RYAN. The tavern is hushed. The air is so still the cigar smoke rises straight up to the ceiling. Creating a mystic gulf, soon to be pierced by the shining tip of Ryan's dart as he prepares a soon-to-be-legendary toss in the annals of the county league. (*Just as he is about to throw the dart, Mrs. Harrigan enters, spoiling his shot.*)

MRS. HARRIGAN. (*Shrill.*) Monsignor Ryan! We've got a problem in the kitchen!

MSGR. RYAN. Good God, Mrs. Harrigan! Can't you enter a room without launching a vocal assault on everyone in it!

MRS. HARRIGAN. I'm sorry. I didn't think you were doing anything important.

MSGR. RYAN. The game of darts, Mrs. Harrigan, is very important. Besides being a noble pursuit, it is a vital part of the social fabric of our community. As shepherd of this fold, it is my duty to maintain close contact with the ways of my flock. Now, get lost. I've got a major tournament coming up in a couple of weeks.

MRS. HARRIGAN. But, Monsignor. What about the problem in the kitchen?

MSGR. RYAN. (*With patience tested.*) And what problem would that be, Mrs. Harrigan?

MRS. HARRIGAN. Tipples Nolan turned up at the back door a little while ago to mooch a cup of coffee. Now he's asking if he can have a few minutes with you. I don't

7

think I can get him to leave on my own.

MSGR. RYAN. Probably looking to put the touch on me again, I suppose. Hmmm. What state is he in?

MRS. HARRIGAN. Well, his knees haven't buckled yet.

MSGR. RYAN. Well, it is a little early in the day. Even for Tipples. All right, Mrs. H. Send him in.

MRS. HARRIGAN. (*Turning away, then turning back.*) Yes, Sir. Oh, and Father Connally called from the station, Monsignor. About ten minutes ago. Said he was coming straight here.

MSGR. RYAN. Is he? Good, good. Let's see if we can't get Tipples on his way before he gets here.

MRS. HARRIGAN. (*Exiting hurriedly.*) Yes, sir! (*Msgr. Ryan arranges chairs, setting the stage for his audience with Tipples Nolan.*)

MSGR. RYAN. Now, see here Tip. If you think I'm going to be conned into financing another one of your drinking jags, you've got another thing coming. (*The telephone rings.*) What now? Mrs. Harrigan! Could you pick up the extension, please? (*The ringing continues.*) Silly me. Expecting the poor girl to walk and chew gum at the same time. (*He answers the phone.*) Contrition parish. Monsignor Ryan speaking. Oh, hello Mrs. Leahy ... I'm fine, thank you ... What's on your mind? (*Mrs. Harrigan ushers in the inebriated Tipples Nolan, negotiates him into a chair, then exits. Tipples dozes.*) Easy now ... Easy, now Mrs. Leahy, please. Now, you and I both know that you're the furthest person from damnation that ever lifted a telephone ... Mrs. Leahy, I honestly don't think that attending two evenings of bingo in the course of a week constitutes a gambling addiction ... and I can assure you that God has never damned a soul for playing a good Catholic game like bingo ... Absolutely ... It's my pleasure ... G'bye, Mrs. Leahy. (*He hangs up, looks at the now dozing Tipples, then tries waking him gently.*) Tip. Hey, Tip. (*A beat, then he shouts.*) Another round for the bar!

TIPPLES. (*Springing to life, and from his chair.*) Same again, Joseph! Oh. Hello, Monsignor.

MSGR. RYAN. Hello, Tip. I hope I haven't kept you

waiting too long.

TIPPLES. Not at all. I just got here.

MSGR. RYAN. (*Maneuvering him into the chair.*) Good. Good. Have a seat. What can I do for you, Tip?

TIPPLES. Monsignor. Do you remember the time you bet me a ten spot that I couldn't quit drinking?

MSGR. RYAN. Like it was yesterday.

TIPPLES. Well, I've come to collect.

MSGR. RYAN. Huh?

TIPPLES. I've forsaken the bottle.

MSGR. RYAN. You have?

TIPPLES. Loosed myself from the clutches of demon rum.

MSGR. RYAN. As I recall, Tip, your tastes run more along the lines of John Barleycorn.

TIPPLES. Well, John and I are friends no more.

MSGR. RYAN. After all you've been through together?

TIPPLES. You can't let sentimental attachments stand in the way of spiritual renewal, Monsignor

MSGR. RYAN. Oh, amen to that Tip. Amen. And just where along the road to Damascus were you slain by Providence?

TIPPLES. Eh?

MSGR. RYAN. When did the Almighty grace you with your beatific vision?

TIPPLES. Come again?

MSGR. RYAN. When did you swear off the sauce, Tip?

TIPPLES. Oh, last night at Reilly's. Just around closing time.

MSGR. RYAN. This wouldn't be a hasty vow taken while kneeling before the porcelain shrine, would it?

TIPPLES. No, Sir. I haven't taken antibuse in years. I just made a decision and I'm sticking to it.

MSGR. RYAN. Ah, you're a good man, Tip. Now, don't take this the wrong way. But you seem to be a bit further into your cups than one might expect of a man who's been on the wagon since last night.

TIPPLES. Oh, well. Heh, heh. You see, Reilly insisted that I come by today. Just to raise a few glasses in celebration of my pledge.

MSGR. RYAN. I see. I see.

TIPPLES. I didn't want to be rude.

MSGR. RYAN. Of course not.

TIPPLES. Reilly's too nice a fella to have his feelings hurt.

MSGR. RYAN. Spoken like a true Christian, Tip.

TIPPLES. Thank you, Monsignor.

MSGR. RYAN. Now about our little wager. Just to add a little extra incentive to your effort, what do you say to double or nothing that you don't stay on the wagon for a whole year?

TIPPLES. (*Caught.*) Hmmm. Well, I'm gonna hate to take that kind of coin from you, Padre. But you've got yourself a bet. (*They shake hands as Mrs. Harrigan enters.*)

MSGR. RYAN. Good man. Ah, Mrs. Harrigan. Now I hate to end our visit so soon, Tip. But I've got some business to tend to.

TIPPLES. (*Wandering about in search of an exit.*) Not at all. Not at all. So long, Monsignor!

MSGR. RYAN. So long, Tip! Mrs. Harrigan will see you out. (*Mrs. Harrigan grabs Tipples and steers him toward the door. Msgr. Ryan continues in a loud whisper.*) Mrs. H. Get a sandwich or something into him before he goes.

MRS. HARRIGAN. (*Letting Tipples wander.*) I'm not having him fall asleep in my kitchen again.

MSGR. RYAN. Then set him up in the parish council room.

MRS. HARRIGAN. (*Retrieving Tipples.*) All right. But what about Father Connally?

MSGR. RYAN. I'll look after Father Connally. You just send him in to me when he gets here.

MRS. HARRIGAN. But he is here. (*She and Tipples exit as Fr. Sean Connally squeezes past them into the room, carrying suitcases.*)

MSGR. RYAN. Sean! Where did you come from?

SEAN. Mrs. Harrigan let me slip in through the kitchen. I saw Tipples through the window and didn't want to bother you. How are ya, Father Ryan? I'm sorry

— *Monsignor* Ryan.

MSGR. RYAN. That's okay. I'm not used to the title yet, myself.

SEAN. Well, anyway, congratulations. You deserve it.

MSGR. RYAN. Thank you, my boy, thank you. C'mon now. Put your bags down and humor an old man for a minute. (*He pushes a button on the phone, then shouts toward offstage.*) Mrs. Harrigan! I'm turning the ringer off in here. Will you pick up the calls on the extension, please?

MRS. HARRIGAN. (*Offstage.*) I will, Monsignor!

MSGR. RYAN. (*To Sean.*) I wish I could make book on that. (*He opens a small refrigerator and removes a can of beer.*) How about a cold one, Sean?

SEAN. Not just now, thanks. I'll probably have a few at my father's place later.

MSGR. RYAN. (*Dreamily.*) A tavern in the family. That's gotta be nice.

SEAN. I'll take a soda if you have one in there.

MSGR. RYAN. I do. We run a full service parish here. (*Takes a can of soda from the refrigerator and hands it to Sean.*) So. How's Kelly doin', Sean?

SEAN. Father Kelly? He's fine. Sharp as ever. Said to be sure to give you his best.

MSGR. RYAN. Is he still preaching sacrifice to the affluent?

SEAN. Of course.

MSGR. RYAN. Kelly's being wasted in a suburban outpost like St. Michael's. And from what I hear about you since you've been out of the Sem, so are you, my young friend.

SEAN. Thank you. That goes a long way, coming from you.

MSGR. RYAN. In fact, Sean. I can't help thinking that it's that Foreign Legion assignment that's at the heart of your problem. But let's not get into that right off the bat. We'll have plenty of time for that while you're here.

SEAN. Oh, I don't mind talking about it. That's why I'm here, Right? I can't see where it's the parish that's the

11

problem. In fact, St. Michael's has pointed out a few things for me.

MSGR. RYAN. Such as?

SEAN. Such as, just what is it that we do anyway? We're sure not saving souls, as far as I can see. Everything is so mundane.

MSGR. RYAN. Just because you're not casting demons into the fountain down at the mall doesn't mean you're not having an effect, Sean.

SEAN. And I'm not looking for biblical proportions, believe me. I'd just like to know that I'm making a difference. I'm tired of just going through the motions.

MSGR. RYAN. I think you seriously need to take a closer look at the work that you do.

SEAN. I've looked. Believe me, I've looked. Monsignor, I used to be able to find the divine intent in every stupid chore that was handed to me. I could find God in a bingo chip, I was so fired up.

MSGR. RYAN. Imagine that?

SEAN. I haven't given a single piece of spiritual advice in more than six months. And that was to some guy who was upset over a stolen BMW. The spiritual percentage in our racket has shrunk. It's as if we're just around to keep the faithful entertained so they'll keep forking it over come Sunday. Run a theatre night, beg for money. Throw a dinner dance, beg for money. Run a bus trip to Atlantic City, beg for the money everybody lost while they were on the bus trip to Atlantic City.

MSGR. RYAN. Collections are down all over, Sean. People have to be told.

SEAN. They've been told. I spend so much time preaching about money, I'm thinking of leaving the priesthood and becoming an announcer for Public Broadcasting.

MSGR. RYAN. Sean, I still think you're seriously underestimating the value in those so-called "stupid chores." The social and spiritual health of a parish go hand-in-hand. Not to mention the value of the example you set while associating with your parishioners.

SEAN. I know. Father Kelly says the same thing. I just can't shake this useless feeling. I hope this scheme of his pans out.

MSGR. RYAN. Well, I've always respected Johnny Kelly's judgement. And if he thinks a little time on your home turf might help you sort things out, that's good enough for me. I'm glad to have you.

SEAN. Thanks. I should give Father Byrne a call and thank him, too. It was nice of him to agree to the switch.

MSGR. RYAN. Are you kidding? He jumped at the chance. He's been wanting out of the city for more than a year, now. Between you and me, Sean. The Chancery did neither me nor Father Byrne any favors by assigning him here.

SEAN. Bad casting?

MSGR. RYAN. Oh, he's all right. He's just from a different sort of ... planet. Like your man Kelly says: "You can take a rich boy off the golf course. You can put him in a poolhall ... "

SEAN. "You can chalk his cue for him ... "

BOTH. "But you can't keep him from leaving divots in the felt!" (*They laugh.*)

SEAN. Ah, the wit and wisdom of Father John Aloysius Kelly.

MSGR. RYAN. Says it all about Father Byrne.

SEAN. You wonder how they make these assignments, sometimes.

MSGR. RYAN. (*Tossing a dart.*) With a blindfold, a map, and one of these. You know, I put Byrne in charge of the CYO when he first got here. He took twenty-five boys, who together spend a third-world economy on basketball shoes, and took them to a cricket clinic.

SEAN. Cricket? Aside from being a bit sissified, isn't that a little too British in tone for this neighborhood?

MSGR. RYAN. His mother was English. He thought it would soften the boys' rough edges. And we won't talk about the Union Jack Father Byrne hung up in his room.

SEAN. And the building didn't fall down?

MSGR. RYAN. No. But your father did threaten to burn

13

it down.

SEAN. A master of the tactful response my old man. Hey, will I have the CYO while I'm here?

MSGR. RYAN. You will. But we'll discuss your duties tomorrow. Why don't you take the afternoon and get yourself reacquainted with the neighborhood? (*Mrs. Harrigan returns.*)

SEAN. I'll take you up on that. If I don't drop in on my father today, I'll have my head handed to me.

MRS. HARRIGAN. Excuse me, Fathers. Monsignor, Katy Thompson is on the phone. She's asking to have Father Byrne sent over.

MSGR. RYAN. Hmmm. I'm afraid this is one time when we'll have to let Mrs. Thompson be, Mrs. H. Tell her the new priest will be around to see her in the morning.

SEAN. You're not talking about Peggy Thompson's mother. Are you?

MSGR. RYAN. Peggy Keenan *nee* Thompson, Father Connally.

SEAN. Yes, Sir. It's her then?

MSGR. RYAN. I'm afraid so. Poor woman.

SEAN. What's her trouble?

MSGR. RYAN. The doctors have a lot of medical mumbo-jumbo for it. An obsessive-compulsive disorder brought on by a series of small strokes she's had since the death of her husband. Something like that. The bottom line is that it's all manifested itself in an inability to accept the notion of forgiveness. She's convinced that she's hellbound. Confesses the same meager infractions over and over again as if they were a sure ticket to Hell.

MRS. HARRIGAN. She's turned Confession into an Olympic event. Some say it was Katy Thompson's ramblings that drove Father Byrne out of town.

MSGR. RYAN. Mrs. Harrigan. Father Byrne was not driven out of town. He is taking part in an experimental curate exchange between our parish and St. Michael's out yonder.

MRS. HARRIGAN. Every day these past few months I've been laying out a blue pill and a red pill for him in the

14

morning, And a big gray one for him when he gets back from Katy Thompson's.

MSGR. RYAN. That will be all, Mrs. Harrigan. Tell Mrs. Thompson that Father Connally will be around to see her tomorrow.

SEAN. If you don't mind, Monsignor, I'd rather talk to her now. I wouldn't feel right making her wait. I've known the Thompsons all my life.

MSGR. RYAN. Eagerness is a good sign, Father Connally. Take the call in here. (*He stands.*) Mrs. Harrigan and I will repair to the kitchen for a cup of tea. (*Aside to her, taking her arm.*) And to discuss the party line regarding Father Byrne's absence.

(*They exit. Sean picks up the phone receiver. The stage goes dark but for a light on Sean. Another light reveals Katy Thompson, also on the phone.*)

SEAN. Hello?

MRS. THOMPSON. Hello? Father Byrne?

SEAN. No Ma'am. This is Father Connally. Sean Connally. Remember me?

MRS. THOMPSON. I'm sorry, Father. I don't. The only Sean Connally I remember from around here was a long-haired, scruffy-faced hoodlum my daughter Peggy went with in high school. And he'd never make a priest.

SEAN. (*Embarrassed.*) Yes. Well, I've got a lot of cousins. What can I do for you, Mrs. Thompson? Father Byrne is away for awhile. I'm filling in for him.

MRS. THOMPSON. Father, I need to make my Confession. There's things on my conscience and I'm afraid I might not make it to First Friday.

SEAN. But First Friday was just yesterday, Mrs. Thompson. Didn't Father Byrne just hear your Confession?

MRS. THOMPSON. Well, yes. He did.

SEAN. And what horrible thing could you possibly have done since yesterday?

MRS. THOMPSON. I don't know, Father. I forget

15

everything anymore. I don't do anything 'cause the doctors won't let me. But I'm just so scared all the time. Can't you please come over, Father? Please? (*Lights down on Katy Thompson. Lights up on rectory.*)

SEAN. Easy now, Mrs. Thompson. Easy now ... Of course I'll come over. I can come over right away, if you'd like ... Your daughter will let me in? All right. I'll see you in a little while. (*He hangs up and enters a reverie as Msgr. Ryan returns.*) Peggy, Peggy, Peggy. Peggy Thompson.

MSGR. RYAN. Careful, careful, careful. Father Connally. Her name these days, you'll recall, is Keenan, Keenan, Keenan. Peggy Keenan.

SEAN. (*Chastened.*) Yes, Sir. I know.

MSGR. RYAN. And you also know that she hasn't gotten a fair shake out of life these past few years. Becoming a widow isn't easy at any age. But for a young girl ... You'll find she's not the same girl you used to take to dances.

SEAN. Yes, Sir.

MSGR. RYAN. And she's also not the same girl you used to shatter the Commandments with in her mother's basement. Back when you used to carry that key to their basement door around on that stupid 'I 'Heart' You' keychain.

SEAN. Never go to work for your former confessor.

MSGR. RYAN. You don't need a confessional to get the idea behind a single key on one of those big, stupid 'I 'Heart' You' keychains. And I'm sure I don't have to remind you that you're not the same either. The only reservation I had about you coming here was the possibility of old attachments clouding your vision and keeping you from making a clear assessment of your future.

SEAN. Monsignor.

MSGR. RYAN. Let me finish. There isn't a man in our 'racket' as you call it, who hasn't known ... nostalgia. Now, there's absolutely nothing wrong with a few fond memories. Just step wisely. And whatever you do, don't take advantage of Peg's loneliness in order to test

16

yourself.

SEAN. Monsignor, I think you should know me better than that.

MSGR. RYAN. I'm not assailing your character, Sean. It's just that I've seen that sort of thing happen before. All I'm asking you to do is step wisely. All right?

SEAN. (*Exiting.*) All right.

MSGR. RYAN. Good. (*He opens a desk drawer and removes a bottle of Irish whiskey.*) Mrs. Harrigan!

MRS. HARRIGAN. (*Returning.*) Yes, Monsignor?

MSGR. RYAN. (*Handing her the bottle.*) Take this up and put it on Father Connally's nightstand. He's gonna need it.

MRS. HARRIGAN. (*Knowingly.*) Yes, Monsignor. (*Blackout.*)

(*SETTING: We are now in the living room of the house shared by Katy Thompson and her daughter, Peggy Keenan. It is a small house, of modest proportions in an old urban neighborhood. In addition to standard furnishings, there is a small, portable altar-box in evidence. A rather graphic Sacred Heart picture is propped up against it. There are entrances indicating a front door, a kitchen, and an upstairs portion of the house.*

AT RISE: About half an hour has passed. Peggy Keenan is buzzing about the room in a cleaning frenzy. The doorbell is heard.)

PEGGY. Oh, no. It can't be. Not yet. (*She checks her appearance, answers the door. Billy Thompson enters, carrying a cumbersome bag of laundry.*)

BILLY. Hi, Sister!

PEGGY. (*Flying back to her cleaning.*) She called the priest again!

BILLY. I'm fine. Couldn't be better. Why the big fuss? Father Byrne has seen this place in every state imaginable.

PEGGY. It's not Father Byrne. There's a new priest filling in.

BILLY. A new lamb to the slaughter, huh? Why don't they stop wasting their bench and just send the Archbishop in to deal with Mom?

PEGGY. (*Sheepishly.*) Well, it's not exactly Father Connally's first experience with her.

BILLY. Father who?

PEGGY. Father Connally.

BILLY. Connally.

PEGGY. Uh huh.

BILLY. Father Sean Connally? (*Peggy nods.*) So that's why you're throwing a cleaning fit. Father What-a-waste comes to call!

PEGGY. Billy. What's going on in that warped mind of yours?

BILLY. Nothing that hasn't gone on in yours, I'm sure.

PEGGY. Well knock it off and help me straighten up.

BILLY. What can I do?

PEGGY. One, stop smirking. Two, take Mom's altar box upstairs. She doesn't need that just for Confession.

BILLY. That thing? Uh, uh. Not me. I'm not going near that thing. That picture, and that ... gothic humidor have given me the creeps since the first day they came into this house.

PEGGY. They won't hurt you.

BILLY. I know they won't. 'Cause I'm keeping my distance.

PEGGY. Why?

BILLY. I don't know. It's all so ... it looks like something you're supposed to set up to keep vampires away.

PEGGY. Oh, please!

BILLY. (*Wary of the altar-box.*) I'll bet that picture bleeds when somebody who isn't a regular churchgoer so much as looks at it.

PEGGY. You're nuts.

BILLY. Maybe. But I'm still not going near that thing. (*The doorbell is heard.*) You deal with the port-a-church. I'll get the door. (*Peggy closes the altar-box, picks it up and exits. Billy answers the door and Sean enters.*)

BILLY. Hello, Father Connally!

SEAN. Hey, Billy! How're you doin?

BILLY. Just fine.

SEAN. Going to school?

BILLY. Yeah, part time. I'm on work study at State.

SEAN. Living out there?

BILLY. Yeah, that's the only way I can be close enough to my job. I'm sharing an apartment with a couple of other guys from the program. (*Peggy returns, but Sean doesn't notice.*)

SEAN. Sounds dangerous. Can any of you cook?

BILLY. We're amazingly self-sufficient.

19

PEGGY. Except on laundry day.

SEAN. Hello, Peg.

PEGGY. Hi, Sean.

BILLY. John! Marcia!

PEGGY. (*Handing Billy some cash.*) Billy. Mom wants a candle lit. Run up to the church for her, will you?

BILLY. What's the intention this time?

PEGGY. Daddy's anniversary is next week, smart mouth.

BILLY. I'm sorry, Peg. But if I had a dollar for every candle she's burned for that man, I could skip college and retire.

PEGGY. Billy.

BILLY. Sean, we should have buried the old guy with a shovel in his hands. He could have tunnelled his way out of Purgatory by now.

PEGGY. William.

BILLY. I'm going. But I can't in good conscience leave without first offering the good Father a belt. Papa would have wanted it that way. Whaddaya say to a short one, Reverend?

SEAN. No thanks, Billy. It's a little early for me.

BILLY. That's just what Father Byrne used to say when he first started coming around here.

PEGGY. The candle, little brother?

BILLY. You guys used to just send me for ice cream.

PEGGY. Get out of here!

BILLY. (*Exiting.*) I'm gone. I'm gone. See ya in church!

SEAN. Well, we did used to just send him for ice cream.

PEGGY. Don't flatter yourself, Sean Connally. My mother did ask to have a candle lit.

SEAN. Oh, I would never suspect you of setting us up to be alone, Pegeen.

PEGGY. I should hope not. Not with that Connally reputation for compromising the female population of the parish. (*They share a hug that is just slightly too long for comfort.*)

SEAN. So. How are you, Peg?

PEGGY. I'm fine. Father Connally. And what about you? What brings you back to the city?

SEAN. Oh, I just got a little homesick. My pastor and Monsignor Ryan arranged for me and Father Byrne to swap assignments for a few weeks.

PEGGY. And the Monsignor sent you straight to my mother?

SEAN. Well, I was right there when she called. I couldn't just leave her hanging.

PEGGY. It's not a job for a young man, Sean.

SEAN. Oh, come on.

PEGGY. I'm serious. Even when the Monsignor came down here himself that time —

MRS. THOMPSON. (*Offstage.*) Peggy!

PEGGY. Just a minute, Mom!

SEAN. He didn't tell me he'd been down here.

PEGGY. I'm not surprised. After that episode.

MRS. THOMPSON. (*Offstage.*) Peggy! Who are you talking to?

PEGGY. It's Sean Connally, Mom!

MRS. THOMPSON. (*Offstage.*) That scruffy guttersnipe! Get him and his mangy head out of here, Peggy! I won't have him in this house when the new priest gets here!

PEGGY. I said *Father* Connally, Mom!

MRS. THOMPSON. (*Offstage.*) Oh! Why didn't you tell me he was here? He'll be thinking I have no manners! I'll be right down, Father!

PEGGY. I'd better make myself scarce.

SEAN. Wait a minute. Tell me about the Monsignor.

PEGGY. It wasn't much of anything. Really. You know how high-strung he can be.

SEAN. But —

PEGGY. Sorry, Sean. I took a vow. (*She exits toward the kitchen as Mrs. Katy Thompson enters from upstairs.*)

MRS. THOMPSON. Hello, Father.

SEAN. Hello, Mrs. Thompson. It's good to, umm, meet you. It's always nice to put a face to a voice. Why don't we have a seat and talk about what's bothering you. (*They sit.*)

MRS. THOMPSON. Oh, Father. I'm all mixed up.

SEAN. You and me both. What are you mixed up about.

MRS. THOMPSON. Well ... what some people say isn't a sin, I think is a sin, and I can't stand thinking about sins, because then I feel like I'm committing a sin, and I can't afford any more sins at my age. Father ... I've been bad.

SEAN. All right, Mrs. Thompson. Come clean. Have you been meeting sailors down at Murphy's West End?

MRS. THOMPSON. Oh, what do I do except sit around here all day thinking?

SEAN. I don't know. You tell me. What do you think about?

MRS. THOMPSON. Oh ... just things.

SEAN. What sorts of things?

MRS. THOMPSON. Things I shouldn't be thinking about.

SEAN. Can you give me a for instance?

MRS. THOMPSON. I ... Oh, Father. How can I tell you?

SEAN. Just say it straight out. I can take it.

MRS. THOMPSON. Well. One of the neighbor's sons got married last month. And you know how after the wedding, the bride and groom go off together? You know what happens?

SEAN. They count up the money in their wedding envelopes?

MRS. THOMPSON. No, no. After that. Later on ... in bed ... You know what happens?

SEAN. I've heard stories. At Baptisms.

MRS. THOMPSON. Is it a sin to have it come to mind, Father?

SEAN. You can't stop things from popping into your head, Mrs. Thompson. And everybody at a wedding knows that's going to happen. It's not a secret. Besides, isn't that what everybody wants them to do? So they'll have babies? Keep their families and the Church growing?

MRS. THOMPSON. (*Rapid fire.*) But Father, when I start thinking about things like that, I can't stop thinking about them. And then I get myself all flustered and

22

nervous, and then I start bothering people with questions about whether something is a sin or not, and getting everybody mad at me because no matter how many people tell me I have nothing to worry about, I still worry, and then I feel like I'm committing a sin because I can't even believe the priest when he tells me I have nothing to worry about, and if you fellas don't know, who does? And then I get scared that God will be mad at me, and I can't afford to have God mad at me, because any one of us could die at any moment, and if I died while God was mad at me, I'd never see my husband again, because he'd be candled out of Purgatory and I'd be sinned into Hell. (*Beat. _ Beat.*) Father?

SEAN. (*Dazed.*) Yes?

MRS. THOMPSON. It's nothing to say "Hell" when you're just talking about the place and not wishing somebody was in it, is it?

SEAN. No. No, Mrs. Thompson. It's nothing.

MRS. THOMPSON. Will you hear my Confession, Father?

SEAN. But Father Byrne heard your Confession just yesterday.

MRS. THOMPSON. I know he did. But I'm not sure I told him everything the way I was supposed to. Please, Father?

SEAN. Okay, Mrs. Thompson. (*Sean prepares, taking a prayer book and a sacramental stole from his pocket. Mrs. Thompson takes a recipe box from a shelf, kneels beside Sean, then removes an index card from the recipe box.*)

MRS. THOMPSON. Ready?

SEAN. I'm ready. Are you ready?

MRS. THOMPSON. I'm ready.

SEAN. Fire away.

MRS. THOMPSON. (*Reading aloud from the index card.*) Bless me Father, for I have sinned. It has been about ... (*She checks a clock.*) Twenty-seven hours since my last Confession. These are my sins. I have argued with my daughter, annoyed my son, and I've gotten two neighbors, three members of the Rosary Society, a Sister of Charity, two Mormon missionaries, and the operator on the call-in TV prayer show cross with me for asking too many questions. For these and all the sins of my past life in the way God sees them, I am truly sorry. Please say that God forgives me, Father.

SEAN. Of course He forgives you, Mrs. Thompson. Now. For your penance, I want you to do something very special. Have you got another one of those index cards handy?

MRS. THOMPSON. (*Handing him a blank card.*) Yes, Father.

SEAN. Do you have a pen in there?

MRS. THOMPSON. (*Producing a pen from the recipe box.*) Surely.

SEAN. (*Copying lines from the prayer book.*) These are a few lines from a psalm that's always been a favorite of mine. I want you to read this aloud anytime you feel yourself beginning to doubt God's forgiveness.

MRS. THOMPSON. (*Stands and reads aloud as Sean hands her the card.*) "I acknowledged my sin to you ... my guilt I covered not ... I said, 'I confess my faults to the Lord' ... and you took away the guilt of my sin." That's all I have to do?

SEAN. That's all.

MRS. THOMPSON. Oh, thank you, Father. Thank you ever so much!

SEAN. No problem. That's why they pay me the big money. (*Beat.*)

MRS. THOMPSON. Father?

SEAN. Yes Ma'am?

MRS. THOMPSON. I'm afraid I forgot to tell you a few things.

SEAN. Mrs. Thompson.

MRS. THOMPSON. Please, Father. Hear my Confession again. I wouldn't feel right starting my penance without feeling that I'd made a clean breast of things. (*Sean gives her a playfully reproachful look. She reads from the card.*) "I acknowledged my sin to you. My guilt I covered not. I said, 'I confess my faults to the Lord.' And you took away the guilt of my sin."

SEAN. And I want you to do it that way every time you start to doubt. As often as it takes.

MRS. THOMPSON. (*Relieved.*) Yes, Sir. Thank you, Father. Thank you ever so much.

SEAN. Anytime.

MRS. THOMPSON. (*Shouts toward kitchen.*) Peggy!

PEGGY. (*Offstage.*) Yes, Mom?

MRS. THOMPSON. Come keep Father company! I have to go upstairs and practice my penance!

PEGGY. (*Offstage.*) Okay, Mom!

MRS. THOMPSON. Thanks again, Father.

SEAN. My pleasure.

MRS. THOMPSON. (*Turns to leave, then turns back.*) Father?

SEAN. Yes?

MRS. THOMPSON. (*Exits quickly, reading from the card.*) I acknowledged my sin to you ... (*Peggy returns.*)

SEAN. Can I have that drink now?

PEGGY. I'd say you've earned it. What does the rest of your day look like? (*She pours whiskeys as Sean picks up a photo album and starts thumbing through it.*)

SEAN. Nothing much. Just a walk around the neighborhood. I have to stop in and see my father later. Has the parish changed much?

PEGGY. A bit. In the market for a tour guide?

SEAN. That'd be great. You're sure it's no bother?

PEGGY. (*Handing Sean a drink.*) Are you kidding? Oh, Lord. My mother's been going through the old photo albums again.

SEAN. Hey, the prom. You were the most beautiful girl there that night, Peg. I can still hear the guys. "I can't believe he's gonna be a priest. A babe like that on his arm and he's gonna be a freakin' priest." That was some night.

PEGGY. All thirty-six hours of it.

SEAN. I thought my old man was going to kill me.

PEGGY. I can still hear my mother. "Peggy. You didn't provide Sean with any tall tales of his former sinfulness to impress his fellow seminarians with, did you?"

SEAN. You never told me she asked you that!

PEGGY. Because you would have come clean and gotten us both killed. Once you got religion you developed a conscience the size of a house. We kept our mouths shut and no harm came of it. You went into the seminary ... I met Bobby ... (*She begins to cry softly.*) And life went on.

SEAN. How are you doing in that respect, Peg?

PEGGY. I'm okay. You marry a cop, you take your chances.

SEAN. Come on, Peg. Being a cop in this town was always considered a good job.

PEGGY. (*Uncomfortably.*) Yeah. Well, like I said. The neighborhood's changed a bit. I need some ice. I'll be right back.

SEAN. (*Making an attempt.*) Ice in your whiskey? Fine Irish girl you turn out to be.

PEGGY. Maybe I'm a half-breed and my parents just never told me. No ice for you, then?

SEAN. For the son of a barkeep? I'd be a disgrace to the family name.

PEGGY. (*Forcing a giggle.*) Okay. (*She exits toward kitchen.*)

SEAN. I'm gonna have enough to answer for in the next life without adding iced whiskey to the list. (*Blackout.*)

ACT I, Scene 3

(SETTING: The parish office.

AT RISE: It is now Saturday night. Msgr. Ryan is heard singing offstage. Sean is revealed sitting at the desk, speaking on the phone.)

SEAN. Yeah. You were right, Pop. The neighborhood has seen better days ... Sure ... *(Msgr. Ryan, musing over a small portable chess set, enters and indicates that Sean should vacate the desk.)* Listen, Pop. I've to get going ... I promise ... I'll be by real soon ... I've just been busy settling into the routine around here ... this is a working visit, not a vacation ... uh huh ... Right ... I will ... I'll tell him ... Okay ... So long, Pop ... And thanks for the history lesson. *(Hangs up.)* Monsignor. That was my father. He told me to tell you that he's mad at you.

MSGR. RYAN. What's his gripe now?

SEAN. He says you haven't been by the bar in more than a month, and that if you don't think enough of him to walk two blocks down the street to see him, then you're an orange bishop.

MSGR. RYAN. Your father's not a very understanding man, Sean. There's more than one tavern in this parish. And it's my duty as pastor to make the rounds and see to it that they're all maintaining the proper moral tone.

SEAN. Been winning at darts again, haven't you?

MSGR. RYAN. Haven't paid for a drink since St. Patrick's Day. And then only because my reflexes were a little bit dulled by the bad weather. I'm ahead for the first time in a long time. And I'm not going to ruin my streak by walking into your father's establishment. The man is a hustler.

SEAN. That's a far cry from a dart board you've got there.

MSGR. RYAN. *(Venomously.)* This nonsense. The trappings of office.

SEAN. How so?

MSGR. RYAN. (*While grabbing a snack from a nearby stash.*) You see, Sean. As a lowly priest and pastor, confining my leisure activities to the piercing of the cork was fine. Unfortunately, along with the exalted title of Monsignor comes an association with the Archbishop not unlike your average executive's association with his boss. When I leave here and go to the Chancery, I am transformed. From top dog, to bootlicker. A Grade-A underling. And, as such, I've found it advantageous to familiarize myself with a few of the old boy's more lovingly-held fascinations. Things like this. Things the Archbishop calls 'games of refinement.' Loosely translated, that means 'things that aren't any fun.'

SEAN. Not your speed, huh?

MSGR. RYAN. Maybe it's a flaw in my otherwise sterling character, but I just can't imagine having a few drinks and playing some chess. I can imagine having a few drinks *because* of playing chess. But I just don't find the game relaxing. I don't know. Maybe if I knew it better I'd enjoy it more.

SEAN. That could be. How's your game coming?

MSGR. RYAN. Well, I've just about broken myself of the habit of asking His Excellency to crown me every time I get a man to his side of the board.

SEAN. Who's winning this one?

MSGR. RYAN. I think I've managed to stalemate myself.

SEAN. You don't seem far enough along for that.

MSGR. RYAN. You don't get very far when you keep forgetting which way the pieces move. You know something about chess?

SEAN. Enough to hold my own for awhile. That's about it.

MSGR. RYAN. That's close enough for jazz. C'mon. Sit down and give me some pointers. You can offer it up for your sins. (*He prepares the board; chess is played through the end of the scene.*) So, uh, how did it go with, Katy Gallagher?

SEAN. Katy Thompson *nee* Gallagher.

MSGR. RYAN. Oh, right.

SEAN. It went okay, I guess. Monsignor ... why didn't you tell me you'd been down to see her yourself?

MSGR. RYAN. Who told you that?

SEAN. Peggy let it slip.

MSGR. RYAN. What is the Faith coming to when you can't even silence a young woman with the threat of excommunication?

SEAN. Why did you keep it to yourself?

MSGR. RYAN. Well ... as you've probably found out, it's not exactly an experience that lends itself well to description. You kind of have to be there.

SEAN. I'll give you that. She's scared silly that she'll never see her husband again.

MSGR. RYAN. If she wants to see that poor soul again, she'd better get down to some serious blasphemy. The late Mr. Thompson wasn't exactly the moral cornerstone of the parish.

SEAN. So I understand. My father was just telling me that he and Mr. Thompson used to run around a lot together in their younger days.

MSGR. RYAN. Oh, that they did. No offense, Sean. But I know from those days. Neither of them ever really stopped running around.

SEAN. I know that. If my old man had given it even a little bit of a rest, he and my mother wouldn't be living on opposite ends of the state right now.

MSGR. RYAN. Don't be too hard on him, Sean. Marriage slowed him down more than it has a lot of other men ... or women these days, for that matter. Not to defend any extramarital habits he may have had ... but compared to Dan Thompson's behavior beyond the altar, your father was an anchorite.

SEAN. Did Mrs. Thompson know?

MSGR. RYAN. Of course, she knew. The whole parish knew. But Katy came from very old-fashioned stock. She'd never have had the nerve to walk the way your mother did. She was raised on the notion that a woman needed to be able to take whatever a man dished out to her. To stand close, no matter how big a rat he turned out

29

to be. And maybe "rat" is too strong a word. Dan's father and grandfather were much the same, I'm told. As far as Dan knew, that was how men lived their lives. He did as he pleased and his wife just had to understand that he had a bit of a wild streak.

SEAN. And she's still carrying the torch.

MSGR. RYAN. More than one. There are over one-hundred votive candles in our sanctuary. On any given day, at least half of them are burning for Dan Thompson.

SEAN. You're kidding.

MSGR. RYAN. Word of honor. Social Security in action. It was the frequency of Mrs. Thompson's custom that allowed us to switch over to those new electric candles.

SEAN. Monsignor. There's something else I've just gotta ask you.

MSGR. RYAN. (*Indicating chess board.*) Wait a minute. Which way does the rocket ship move?

SEAN. Diagonally. And it's called a "bishop".

MSGR. RYAN. (*Moving his piece.*) It moves diagonally. And it's called a "bishop". That figures. C'mon, c'mon. Your move.

SEAN. Sir. Is it true that you took a leave of absence after the time you counseled Mrs. Thompson?

MSGR. RYAN. (*Annoyed and embarrassed.*) Yes. Yes, Sean. I did. Why do you ask?

SEAN. I'm just trying to understand a few things. I mean ... you've been in the trenches a long time. What upset you so much?

MSGR. RYAN. Be kind, Sean. Don't forget, I'm a local boy, just like you. Katy Thompson is a contemporary of mine. An old friend, in fact. And exactly the same age. To tell you the truth, she frightened me. There but for the grace of God go I and such.

SEAN. That must have been scary ... Monsignor, I know I'm on thin ice here. So feel free to tell me to take a hike. But I have to ask ... or rather ... my father just told me about a prospective seminarian that used to be in the same crowd with him and Dan Thompson.

30

MSGR. RYAN. He did, did he? God bless him.

SEAN. Uh, yeah. And about a fistfight between Dan Thompson and this guy over a girl named Katy Gallagher.

MSGR. RYAN. What are you driving at, Father Connally?

SEAN. I'm not sure, Sir. Like I said, I'm just trying to understand a few things.

MSGR. RYAN. All right, Sean. Not that it's any of your business, but yes. Yes, I once courted Katy Gallagher. Yes, I thought she was too good for Dan Thompson. Yes, Dan and I mixed it up over her. And, if you must know, he clobbered me. But that is neither here nor there. The important part of the story, as far as you're concerned, is that I worked it out. I made my peace. (*Beat.*) Sean. Word of an arm-in-arm stroll between you and Peggy has come to my attention.

SEAN. Good old Mrs. Harrigan. I didn't realize that snitching on the children of parishioners was still one of her hobbies.

MSGR. RYAN. Then it's true?

SEAN. It is.

MSGR. RYAN. And do you think that sort of thing is wise? What did I tell you about proximity to Peg?

SEAN. It was innocent enough.

MSGR. RYAN. Innocence is a wide field, Sean. I remember thinking that the attentions I paid Katy were nothing but innocent flirtation. Until the day they got me a broken nose.

SEAN. Monsignor, this really isn't that big a deal.

MSGR. RYAN. C'mon, Sean. I'll lay even money that there are emotions festering inside you that you are conveniently ignoring.

SEAN. My conscience is perfectly clear.

MSGR. RYAN. So was mine. Until I connected with the business end of Dan Thompson's arm. Sean, the effect of a woman on a man is a deceptively fierce thing. Even for guys like us. Especially for guys like us. The ones with the perfect alibi. Unfortunately, we can tend to forget that our priestly powers don't include absolute resistance to the forces of nature. We remain men. And, as all men do, we have to deal honestly with ourselves when it comes to women. Right?

SEAN. Yes, Sir.

MSGR. RYAN. Magnetism is called a force for a reason.

SEAN. Yes, Sir.

MSGR. RYAN. Is any of this sinking in?

SEAN. Of course it is. But honestly, I am in perfect control of the situation.

MSGR. RYAN. Sean, the minute a guy in our line thinks he's in control of a situation like yours, he might as well take whatever marbles he hasn't lost yet and go play with them out in the middle of the highway.

SEAN. (*Attempting levity.*) Well, I don't know from marbles. Aside from chess, curb-ball was always my game.

MSGR. RYAN. What we are talking about, Father Connally, is not a mere game. It is a gamble. A gamble against all sensible odds. (*Beat.*) But there's no use talking sense to a man bent on making a fool of himself. Now, c'mon and show me some more about this scintillating pastime. Which way do the horses move again?

SEAN. They're not called horses. They're called "knights."

MSGR. RYAN. That's a silly name for them! You can see as plain as day that they're horses!

SEAN. Curb-ball is a lot easier. I don't suppose it's considered a game of refinement, though.

MSGR. RYAN. Curb-ball is fun, right?

SEAN. Right.

MSGR. RYAN. (*Moving a piece.*) Then it is not a game of refinement. Now, shut up and crown me. (*Blackout.*)

ACT I, Scene 4

(*SETTING: The Thompson living room.*

AT RISE: A few weeks have passed. It is late Thursday afternoon. Peggy is discovered sitting on the sofa. She holds in her hand a key, suspended from the I "heart" you keychain mentioned earlier. She is contemplating the keychain, lost in memory, when Billy enters from the kitchen, carrying a full laundry bag.)

BILLY. Thanks for the lunch and laundry, Sis. I'll give you a call over the weekend.

PEGGY. You're leaving already?

BILLY. I have to. We've got some dates coming over tomorrow night. I've got to shovel my share of the apartment.

PEGGY. (*Rising.*) Slobs. One look at that tar pit and the poor girls'll turn to stone. Give me a second and you can drop me off at the church.

BILLY. Let me guess: candles.

PEGGY. (*Gathering her keys, wallet, etc.*) Bright boy. You must be a college student.

BILLY. You know, we could just tell her all those candles get lit and do something really useful with the money.

PEGGY. Like what?

BILLY. We could get lit!

PEGGY. They're going to have to set fire to a candle factory for your soul someday, little brother. (*She indicates "the key".*) Do you still need this key to the basement door?

BILLY. Nah, that's okay. I had that one copied, too. I wish I could figure out what I did with my keys.

PEGGY. If you don't find them while you're excavating your apartment, let me know. We should probably change the locks.

BILLY. Yeah, I suppose so. (*Sean's voice is heard*

33

offstage.)

SEAN. (*Offstage.*) But Mrs. Thompson, you have no sins!

BILLY. How long has he been up there with her this time?

PEGGY. I'm not sure. What time did you get here?

BILLY. I don't know. Forty or fifty minutes ago.

PEGGY. Oh, my God. He's been up there over two hours.

BILLY. (*Amazed.*) Two hours alone in a room with Mom's confessions.

PEGGY. (*Too admiringly.*) It's the third time this week he's been here when I got home from work. She starts watching the soap operas in the afternoon and off she goes. He's the most patient man I've ever seen.

BILLY. Yeah? A couple o' more days with that patient and he'll be bouncing off the walls.

PEGGY. Move it, William.

BILLY. I wouldn't leave him here alone with her if I was you. You'll come back and find him with his head in the oven.

PEGGY. Oh, shut up. (*They exit via the front door. Mrs. Thompson enters hurriedly from upstairs. She is followed closely by Sean.*)

SEAN. Mrs. Thompson. Please. Don't run from me. What is it that you're afraid to tell me?

MRS. THOMPSON. Oh, Father, you don't know. I'm afraid to tell you. I'm afraid you won't be able to forgive me.

SEAN. Give me a shot at it at least.

MRS. THOMPSON. But —

SEAN. Please, Mrs. Thompson. Trust me?

MRS. THOMPSON. Well ... you see, Father ... oh, how can I tell you? You see ... when me and my husband were first married ... we were so young ... we didn't have a penny to our name, so ... we were ... we were careful.

SEAN. Careful? About money?

MRS. THOMPSON. About ... children.

SEAN. Oh. Ohhh ... how careful?

34

MRS. THOMPSON. Very.

SEAN. Um, that's not quite what I meant. I mean ... how did you go about it? Being careful, that is.

MRS. THOMPSON. (*Rapid fire.*) Well, at times when I might have, we didn't. When we were sure I couldn't, we did. If I thought I might, most times we didn't. A few times we did, and I thought I was, and prayed for dear life that I wasn't. Of course, if I had been we'd have done our best. And when we wanted to, we did. Make no mistake about that. But at the beginning, Father, we had nothing to call our own. We lived with my people for a year after we got married. Oh, Father, I'm afraid I didn't have enough children. A lot of my friends had six or seven. God must be angry with me for not doing my duty.

SEAN. All right, Mrs. Thompson. It's all right. Now, hush just a second and let me ask you something. When you said that you didn't when you thought you might, was that all you did?

MRS. THOMPSON. What do you mean, Father?

SEAN. (*Increasingly uncomfortable.*) I mean ... did you ever go further than doing nothing when you thought something might happen?

MRS. THOMPSON. I don't understand?

SEAN. Was the drugstore ever involved, Mrs. Thompson?

MRS. THOMPSON. Was the ...? Oh! Ohhh! Oh, no, Father ... I swear ... I mean, I don't swear ... I ... Father, I'd never even think of such a thing. I wouldn't have even known what to ask for. Though I imagine Dan probably would have. But Father, I promise you, we never did anything like that.

SEAN. Then you've got nothing to worry about. The Church understands that people may have reasons for putting off having children. Or for putting some space between them. Or even for keeping their families to a size that's manageable for them. Needing to be careful, or thinking that you should be, isn't the problem. It's the way people go about it that's the problem. What you and your husband did is perfectly in keeping with the Church's teachings on the matter.

MRS. THOMPSON. It wasn't a sin?

SEAN. It wasn't even a "no no."

MRS. THOMPSON. And God isn't angry with me?

SEAN. He's a busy Man. I doubt He even remembers it.

MRS. THOMPSON. Oh, Father, you always make me feel so good about things. Sometimes, I wish you weren't a priest. My Peggy could use a level-headed fella like you. She's a worrier.

SEAN. Is she?

MRS. THOMPSON. Yes, poor thing. But with a fella like you, she'd soon stop her ... oh ... oh, my ... oh, Father ... I hope you didn't take that ... I hope I didn't embarrass you, or insult you. Honestly, I didn't mean it like I meant about the neighbor boy's wedding. Oh! God'll be thinking I was trying to steal one of his own! "I acknowledged my sin to you. My guilt I covered not." (*She exits, reciting.*)

SEAN. (*Preparing to leave.*) There's got to be an easier way to make a living. (*Peggy returns.*)

PEGGY. Hi.

SEAN. Oh. Hi.

PEGGY. Is something wrong?

SEAN. Oh, no. I'm fine. Peg, I'm sorry about your mother.

PEGGY. Why? There's nothing you can do about it.

SEAN. That's what I mean. I haven't been very much help.

PEGGY. Sean, you're not supposed to be a magician.

SEAN. I don't seem to be much of anything.

PEGGY. Will you stop? I won't have you talking that way about yourself.

SEAN. Why not? It's true. Where does God get off sending the like of me into that poor woman's life? He's her Savior. Let Him do something about it.

PEGGY. Sean. I know I couldn't even pass the physical for the seminary, but aren't you guys supposed to be acting as proxy for Him?

SEAN. Yeah. Supposedly. I'm supposed to be His

instrument. His tool. If this is what He calls using me to fix things, He must have lost the instruction manual.

PEGGY. Sean, don't give up on us now. You're the closest thing to sanity this house has seen in a long time. And I, for one, am very glad you turned up. (*An awkward silence.*) So. I hear the parish is buzzing.

SEAN. What about?

PEGGY. It seems we're an item.

SEAN. Dear, sweet woman that Mrs. Harrigan. A couple of walks around the neighborhood and she thinks it's *The Thorn Birds.*

PEGGY. She is timeless. Telling on us like we were still teenagers. It's like she's frozen in time.

SEAN. Yeah. Lucky her.

PEGGY. What do you mean?

SEAN. Just that it's probably nice not to have to worry about what's coming next in life.

PEGGY. I don't know. I think it would be pretty boring.

SEAN. Maybe. But it'd be a lot safer.

PEGGY. Sean Connally, I believe my mother is beginning to rub off on you.

SEAN. I'm not talking about Judgement Day boxscores. I'm just talking about the normal progress of life. And the things people get swept up in as a result of the decisions they make along the way.

PEGGY. What about it?

SEAN. Every decision we make affects somebody else. Sometimes insignificantly. Sometimes even unnoticeably. But somehow, somebody else is affected. And when someone is greatly affected, well ... sometimes the aftermath of a decision makes you wish that you had just frozen yourself in time. I know I've felt like that.

PEGGY. (*Sensing danger.*) Sean, maybe you'd better not say any more.

SEAN. I haven't been able to sleep very well these past few nights, Peg. I keep thinking about how you cried at my ordination. My mother cried, too, but ... but it was different with you. You weren't happy for me.

PEGGY. Sean, we've been very good about keeping away from this subject.

SEAN. Peg, I've carried the sight of those tears around with me for years now. I see lovers walking: I see you crying. I baptize a baby: I see you crying. There have been times when I'd have done just about anything to get you off my mind. Then, I heard about your engagement. I flew into a jealous rage. Because I couldn't see you crying, anymore. 'At least she's off my conscience,' I said to myself. And I did a pretty good job believing myself for awhile. Then, Bobby got shot ... and there you were again. I was as sorry to see you come back as I was to see you go. I just can't help thinking that I could have saved you a lot of unhappiness, Peg.

PEGGY. (*Trying to keep it light.*) You could've, and you would've, and maybe you should've. But you didn't. So what? You're right about decisions, Sean. We all make them. And we all have to live with them.

SEAN. I've never made a harder decision than that one.

PEGGY. I did have some pretty stiff competition.

SEAN. Please, don't joke about it, Peg.

PEGGY. Sean, I *really* think we should change the subject.

SEAN. I think about you all the time lately, Peg.

PEGGY. Sean, don't.

SEAN. Sometimes, I'd give anything to have that choice to make over.

PEGGY. Please, don't do this.

SEAN. Peg, you've got to let me say it.

PEGGY. Why? Why should I? How can you come back here after all this time, after all that's happened, and say these things to me? You're supposed to *hear* confessions in this house, Father Connally, not make them!

SEAN. Peg, listen. Please.

PEGGY. No! I will not go through all this again! Why couldn't you have just stayed a memory?

SEAN. For the same reason I probably can't stay a priest.

PEGGY. Oh no. No. Don't even think of trying to put that one over on me. I know you, Sean. And you and I both know there's not an ounce of truth to that. It's because you're a priest, safe in your little men's club, that you can say things like that.

SEAN. Peg, you're not being fair.

PEGGY. I'm not being fair? You throw a monkey wrench into my life, and I'm not being fair?

SEAN. I didn't come back here to fight with you. Or to do anything else with you. I came back here to find a misplaced vocation, because I was afraid it was gone for good.

PEGGY. Well, you're not going to find it hanging around here! (*A few beats as they face each other down.*)

SEAN. (*Resigned.*) You're right. I'd better get out of here.

PEGGY. That's probably best. Thanks for coming over to see Mom.

SEAN. That's okay. Anytime. She seems a little flushed today. Is everything all right?

PEGGY. She's coming down with something. That's probably why she called you. If she gets a hangnail, she thinks she's at death's door. If she is sick, she'll be calling you every day until she's over it.

SEAN. That's okay. Really. The only thing that bothers me is the thought of her getting up and down out of bed to let me in. She'll only make herself sicker.

PEGGY. You don't have to come over every time. Just talk to her on the telephone.

SEAN. I've tried that. She doesn't trust the quality of telephone absolution.

PEGGY. I guess you could call me at work if she calls you. I could duck out a little while, come home and let you in. No, that won't work. I can't guarantee being able to break away. (*She notices "the key", picks it up and hands it to him.*) Why don't you take this. It's a spare key to the basement door.

SEAN. Oh, really?

PEGGY. Uh, huh. You can just let yourself in if she

calls.

SEAN. What would your mother say if she knew that scruffy-faced Connally hoodlum had a key to her basement door?

PEGGY. I don't know. Besides, I haven't seen him around here in years.

MRS. THOMPSON. (*Offstage.*) Peggy! Peggy, is that you down there?

PEGGY. (*Shouts toward offstage, then turns to Sean.*) I'll be right up, Mom! Mind letting yourself out?

SEAN. Of course not.

PEGGY. (*Kissing him on the cheek.*) Thanks again for being so sweet to her. Goodbye.

SEAN. G'bye. (*Peggy starts up the stairs, then turns back toward Sean.*)

PEGGY. Sean?

SEAN. Yeah?

PEGGY. Sometimes ... when she's sick like this, she calls Father Byrne in the middle of the night. I mean, sometimes he comes to see her, sometimes he's just too tired. You know ... Feel free to tell her to wait 'til morning if she calls.

SEAN. Okay. If she calls, I'll see how I feel. It's not like I have to walk very far. If I do have to let myself in ... I'll try not to disturb you.

PEGGY. Okay. I'll leave the basement light on for the next few nights. Just in case.

SEAN. Good deal.

PEGGY. G'bye.

SEAN. G'bye, Peg. (*Peggy exits upstairs, Sean lingers.*)

SEAN. (*Addressing God.*) You're not going to make this even a little bit easy for me, are You? (*Blackout.*)

ACT II, Scene 1

(*SETTING: We are in a tavern, owned and operated by Sean's father, Joseph Connally. It is a plain, old-time drinking bar.*

AT RISE: It is now late Thursday night. Connally and Msgr. Ryan and Tipples are discovered. Connally is behind the bar. Msgr. Ryan is lining up a shot at a dart board. Tipples is asleep at the bar.)

CONNALLY. (*Needling.*) Don't give in to the pressure now, Francis. It's only your archdiocesan reputation on the line.

MSGR. RYAN. The finals aren't for two weeks yet.

CONNALLY. Blow this one and you'll be ashamed to show your face at the finals. I should think you'd be able to hit at least one bull's eye out of five on a bet.

MSGR. RYAN. You're dead meat this time, Connally. (*He throws and misses.*) Damnation!

CONNALLY. Ha, ha! Buy me a drink, handsome! We'll stand Tipples a round in the next life.

MSGR. RYAN. Blast it!

CONNALLY. You know what it is, don't you? It's all that chess you've been playing down at the chancery. You're losing touch with the native traditions of your own parish.

MSGR. RYAN. Just set 'em up.

CONNALLY. You are an ungracious host. C'mon. Ask me what I'll have.

MSGR. RYAN. What'll you have, Joseph?

CONNALLY. (*Draws beers and produces an expensive-looking bottle of whiskey.*) And a fascinating question it is, too. Let's see ... I think I'll pour myself something cold. And something costly. I know you wouldn't begrudge me a small glass of the twelve year-old. Just to cut the cold of the beer, mind you. It's a breezy night. I wouldn't want to catch one of those Springtime viruses.

41

MSGR. RYAN. I should never have listened to that son of yours. I'm going to call every parish in the archdiocese. He'll be saying sunrise Masses for the rest of his life.

CONNALLY. And what son might that be? I have given my son up to the Lord. As willingly as Abraham would have smote Isaac. Ah, Abraham and Isaac. If Isaac had been anything like my Sean, Abraham would have stabbed him *and* the angel that tried to stop him. (*Sean walks in on the tail end of the above. He looks disheveled, as he has been wandering for several hours. Noticing Msgr. Ryan, he turns to leave. Sean is noticed by Connally.*)

CONNALLY. Miracle of miracles, will you look who's here! Monsignor, kill the fatted keg!

MSGR. RYAN. (*Going behind bar.*) Don't mind if I do.

CONNALLY. Yes, kill the fatted keg! Put a fine robe on him. (*Puts a barman's apron over Sean's shoulders, takes a pretzel from a bowl on the bar and puts it on Sean's finger.*) And put a ring on his finger! It's the prodigal son returned!

SEAN. Dad.

CONNALLY. Monsignor. Only a few weeks has my son been back in the parish. And do you know what he's done for me in just those few weeks? He didn't just come running down here to see me like any ordinary son of a bartender. Oh, no! And he certainly isn't one of those dotingly devoted visit-once-a-week ingrates, like Matty Campbell's boy Tommy. Not my Sean. He *loves* his father. In the mere few weeks that he's been back, he has honored me with not one, not two, but *three* personally dialed telephone calls. I've been deeply moved, Sean. And I'd be a poor excuse for a father if I didn't say that I'm proud to see a son of mine displaying such an impressive grasp of technology.

SEAN. Dad, will you give it a rest? Monsignor, tell him what a busy man I am.

MSGR. RYAN. (*Insincere.*) Joseph. He's a busy man.

CONNALLY. He's an ass. And I always wanted a girl.

MSGR. RYAN. (*Rising.*) Sorry, Sean. I did my best for

you. (*Indicating Sean.*) I'll leave you, Joseph, to the error of your ways. Sean, I'd appreciate it if you'd take the six-thirty Mass for me tomorrow morning. I'm going to be up late tonight. Making phone calls. Good night, gentlemen! (*He exits.*)

SEAN. What's he in such a mood about?

CONNALLY. I couldn't begin to tell you.

SEAN. You took him again, didn't you?

CONNALLY. (*Drawing a beer for Sean.*) Yes. And it wasn't a pretty sight, Son. I'm just as glad your young eyes weren't around to witness the carnage. So to what do I owe the pleasure? If you don't mind my saying so, you look a little rattled.

SEAN. Me? Nah. I'm fine. Just a little tired. I've been out walking for awhile.

CONNALLY. Okay. Heard from your mother, lately?

SEAN. Yeah. I talked to her last week.

CONNALLY. She doing all right?

SEAN. Sure. You know her. She just got a promotion at work. Says she'll be able to get herself a nicer apartment with the raise she's getting.

CONNALLY. I don't suppose she asked about me.

SEAN. She did. Sends her regards, in fact.

CONNALLY. Great. Regards. How in blazes do you get from 'I will love you and honor you all the days of my life' to 'regards'?

SEAN. By spending too many nights in Atlantic City motel rooms with women who aren't your wife?

CONNALLY. The question was rhetorical.

SEAN. Rhetorical? Have the Gideon's taken to slipping dictionaries into the nightstands next to the Bibles?

CONNALLY. No, wiseguy. I happen to be taking an english course at the state college.

SEAN. You're kidding.

CONNALLY. (*Pulls a textbook from behind the bar.*) I am not. Here's the textbook.

SEAN. Hey, this one's pretty good. I used it myself. What brought this on? You haven't got yourself hooked up with another co-ed, have you?

CONNALLY. Can a priest excommunicate his own father?

SEAN. Not a priest on my level of the totem pole. But an irate son could just forget his collar in the heat of the moment and break a bottle over his father's head.

CONNALLY. In that case, the answer to your question is "No."

SEAN. Pop, what is your problem! I — (*Realizing he is in no position to talk*) I'm sorry, Pop.

CONNALLY. Are you gonna tell me what's wrong? Or are you just gonna sit there and let it eat at you the whole night?

SEAN. I ... uh ... I've developed a little problem since I came back to the parish, Pop.

CONNALLY. What, Monsignor Eagle Eye? He's just blowing off steam.

SEAN. Oh, no. Not him. We get along fine.

CONNALLY. What then? Are you short on money?

SEAN. No. No. This is a tough one, Pop.

CONNALLY. (*Grabbing Sean's drink.*) Sean. Shoot straight with me. Is it this stuff? Are you drinking too much?

SEAN. Not enough.

CONNALLY. Oh, my God, it's a woman! (*He takes the phone off the hook, drags Tipples from his seat, throws him out the door, shuts the door and bolts it.*) Sean, are you crazy? If you think I screwed up, that's nothing compared to what that sort of thing will do to you. It's Peggy, isn't it? You know, some loudmouth was in here the other night saying something about the two of you. I thanked him not to assume that my son is stupid.

SEAN. Yeah, well.

CONNALLY. I always knew there was something up after that prom. How far has this thing gone?

SEAN. Not very.

CONNALLY. How far is "not very"? First base? Second base? Sean, you didn't go and hit a homer, did you?

SEAN. No, Pop. I'm sort of safe at first on an error.

CONNALLY. Thank God for that. At least you've got

some sense. You've got a look on your face like she gave you the key to her chastity belt or something.

SEAN. (*Tossing the key onto the bar.*) Does a key to the basement door count?

CONNALLY. You're trying to kill me, aren't you? You want to leave the priesthood and take over my bar.

SEAN. C'mon, Pop. I need some advice here.

CONNALLY. I'm sorry, Son. But this is a new one on me. I've stood here some nights for hours listening to guys scheming about how they might get their hands on a key like that. I've never come across a fella trying to give one back.

SEAN. You're a bartender. Improvise.

CONNALLY. Hmmm. Okay. What did you say to her?

SEAN. Just that life might have gone a little differently if we'd made other choices along the way.

CONNALLY. Other choices, eh? How did you say it?

SEAN. What do you mean?

CONNALLY. How did you say it? What inflections did you use?

SEAN. How should I know? I didn't have a tape recorder with me. What does that have to do with it, anyway?

CONNALLY. What does it ... ? It has everything to do with it! Women are auditory creatures.

SEAN. They're what?

CONNALLY. Auditory. Didn't they teach you anything in the seminary? How are you supposed to counsel people if you don't even know the fundamental differences between the sexes? Women are auditory by nature. They respond to sound. Like the inflections in a voice. Especially the voice of a man they know they've got a hold on. You've got to watch the tone you take with a woman from 'Good morning' to 'Good night.' Did I ever tell you how I proposed to your mother?

SEAN. How?

CONNALLY. Accidentally.

SEAN. Dad!

CONNALLY. Calm down. I was going to do it

eventually, anyway. But that's not the point. You see, a friend of your mother's had just gotten married, see? Your mother was maid-of-honor, caught the bouquet, the whole nine yards. A week or so afterwards, we were sitting in a soda shoppe having a burger and fries when the wedding comes up in conversation. At some point, your mother said, "Marriage is a wonderful thing." I agreed. A little too fervently, now that I look back on it. But I still should have been all right. A few seconds later. Seconds, mind you. I said, "Helen, will you ... (*He lets his voice trail off.*) Now, I was just trying to decide whether I wanted her to pass me the ketchup or the salt. But the way my voice trailed off when I said "Will you ..." That clinched it for her. She shouted "Yes!", kissed me, hit me up for change and ran to a payphone to call her mother. Inflections, Sean. Watch 'em. They are a man's worst enemy. Got it?

SEAN. (*Humoring his father.*) Got it.

CONNALLY. Hearing is the sense that defines Woman.

SEAN. Right. Thanks, Pop. For a minute there I didn't think you were going to be able to help me. (*Beat.*) You know, my life is going down the toilet pretty fast right now. And I probably don't have time to listen to this. But I've gotta ask. Which sense is it that defines Man?

CONNALLY. Men are visual.

SEAN. Visual.

CONNALLY. Yes, visual. And I'll prove it to you. When you're explaining something to another man, what do you say? You say, "Do you *see* my point" or "Do you *see* what I'm saying." Not "Do you *hear*" or even "Do you *understand*" but "Do you *see*."

SEAN. And women don't do that?

CONNALLY. No, Sir. They say things like, "You *know* I'm right" or "I'm *sure* you agree" or "I *know*, without asking, that you understand."

SEAN. Because they're not visual.

CONNALLY. You got it. That and the fact that not one of them would ever so much as imply that she might be wrong. And I'll give you another example how they're

46

not visual. Women are not affected by pornography.

SEAN. They're not?

CONNALLY. Of course not. You never see women running out to buy magazines full of pictures of naked men.

SEAN. Somebody must read *Playgirl.*

CONNALLY. (*Suggesting homosexuals.*) Oh, somebody does. A couple of "playgirls" sashayed in here last week. I sent them packing fast enough.

SEAN. Why? What did they do?

CONNALLY. I just told you. They came in.

SEAN. You threw customers out just for coming into the bar?

CONNALLY. It was either throw them out myself, or watch a few of my regulars lynch the poor slobs. They must have been crazy coming in here.

SEAN. They probably heard it was a nice place.

CONNALLY. The last thing I need is a reputation for running a "nice" place. Next thing you know, I'll have to be serving mineral water. And wine.

SEAN. Dad —

CONNALLY. I can just see it. A wine bar. A thousand little bottles without a word of English on 'em.

SEAN. Dad —

CONNALLY. A bunch of prissy guys sticking their noses in my glasses and prissin' off about "the bouquet."

SEAN. Pop —

CONNALLY. I'd have to pack up, sell the place, and leave town!

SEAN. Yo, Dad!

CONNALLY. Huh? Oh. I'm sorry, Son. Where were we?

SEAN. Nowhere we need go back to. Listen, Pop. I know it's a low thing to do, not having been around to see you and all. But I'm not very good company tonight. I'm just gonna head back to the rectory.

CONNALLY. Suit yourself. (*Sean goes to leave as Connally spots the key on the bar, picks it up and tosses it to him.*) Hey. Losing the key isn't going to make the door go away.

SEAN. Can my old man turn a phrase, or what? Some of history's greatest philosophers probably stayed awake for weeks to come up with that kind of stuff.

CONNALLY. Never mind that. Just make sure I get a good seat at your unfrocking.

SEAN. I hope it's not a cold day.

CONNALLY. I'll bring you a bar towel.

SEAN. Bring two. It might rain. (*Beat.*)

CONNALLY. (*Concerned.*) Don't be a dope. All right?

SEAN. All right.

CONNALLY. All right. Now get out of here. You're depressing me. (*He opens the door, Tipples falls through.*) Company! See? Now you don't have to worry about me being lonely.

SEAN. Let's get him out of the doorway.

CONNALLY. Nah. Let him be for a minute. If nobody comes to claim him, I'll call the morgue. Get *yourself* out of my doorway, Father Casanova. I run a respectable joint here.

SEAN. (*Exiting.*) I'm gone, I'm gone. See ya in church.

CONNALLY. (*Muttering to himself.*) See ya in church. He'll have to start his own church if he doesn't get himself outta this mess. My son, the television evangelist. Maybe he'll buy me that boat I'm always promising myself. (*He looks down at Tipples.*) Tip. Hey, Tip. Are you still with us? (*He gets a glass from the bar, holds it to Tipples' face, then checks it for fog.*) Well, he's breathing. He can't be that bad. (*He bends down and yells.*) Wake up and sit at the bar like a respectable human being. You lazy souse! (*Tipples springs to life, Connally goes behind the bar.*) So. What brings you out on a fine Thursday night, Tipples?

TIPPLES. Huh?

CONNALLY. To what do I owe this bit of off-night companionship?

TIPPLES. What?

CONNALLY. What'll it be?

TIPPLES. Oh. There you are, Joseph.

CONNALLY. Hello, Tip.

48

TIPPLES. Joseph. Do you remember the time you bet me twenty dollars that I'd never quit drinking? (*Blackout.*)

(*SETTING: The Thompson living room.*

*AT RISE: It is now Friday night. Peggy and Billy
are chatting over a snack.*)

PEGGY. Now wait a minute. You're sure you
followed the directions?

BILLY. Sure, I'm sure. I'm not that dense.

PEGGY. And it was just a plain, straight-forward
chicken recipe?

BILLY. Uh, huh.

PEGGY. Where did you get it?

BILLY. Off the back of the instant soup box I poured
into the stuff.

PEGGY. What kind was it?

BILLY. Generic.

PEGGY. Oh, great. Maybe it was the chicken. You
could've sent somebody to the hospital. (*Billy whistles
conspicuously.*) No.

BILLY. Yeah. Ah, well. There'll be other women.
Next time I'll have to find one with a stronger stomach.

PEGGY. Billy!

BILLY. She's going to be all right. So, can I stay here
tonight?

PEGGY. Of course. It's your house, too. The guys
really won't let you back in the apartment?

BILLY. (*Rubs his head gingerly.*) Not tonight, anyway.

PEGGY. Did they give you that lump on your head?

BILLY. Yeah. Eddie got a little over dramatic and
threw the brass monkeys out the window at me when I
was leaving.

PEGGY. I told you when you moved in with him that
he was a jerk.

BILLY. Ah, it was my own fault. I made a walking
target of myself going out by the window. I should have
used the back stairs.

PEGGY. (*Jumps nervously.*) Did you say you heard

something on the back stairs?

BILLY. No, I said I should have ducked out *my* back stairs. Our apartment is in the front of the building.

PEGGY. Oh. Right.

BILLY. Are you all right?

PEGGY. Sure. Why?

BILLY. I don't know. I thought you seemed a little edgy there, for a minute. So, what kind of night have you been having?

PEGGY. What do you mean by that?

BILLY. In most English-speaking countries, it means "What kind of night have you been having?" Are you sure you're not edgy about something?

PEGGY. (*Edgy.*) I am not edgy.

BILLY. Okay, okay. You're not edgy. Got any plans tonight?

PEGGY. (*Snapping.*) No, I don't have any plans tonight. Why would I have plans? You know I never go out on weeknights.

BILLY. (*Warily.*) I was just making conversation. So, how did Sean make out this afternoon?

PEGGY. What!

BILLY. How did Sean make out with Mom before? Any progress?

PEGGY. Oh. Not really. She's not going to change at this point.

BILLY. I guess not. It's nice of him to keep coming over when she calls. I owe you and Sean an apology, Sis. When he first started coming over here so much, I thought maybe the two of you were just looking to take a roll down Memory Lane together. Seeing everything Sean's tried to do to help Mom ... I feel pretty stupid.

PEGGY. And well you should. You're as bad as Mrs. Harrigan.

BILLY. I know. I'm sorry. Hey, remember how I used to cover for you guys? You're lucky I was a tight-lipped kid.

PEGGY. Tight-lipped? You had to be bought off constantly.

51

BILLY. Ha, ha! Like the time I swiped that key you gave to Sean and threatened to show it to Dad.

PEGGY. Brat.

BILLY. (*Going to where he thinks "the key" should be.*) I remember it like it was yesterday. I snatched it away from him while he was taking off his jacket. Then I held it up by that stupid keychain and — (*Puzzled.*) Did I see you put that key over here yesterday? Or did I get hit on the head too hard?

PEGGY. You got hit on the head too hard.

BILLY. That's usually the safest place to hit me. Anyway, I'm sorry, Peg. I shouldn't have jumped to conclusions.

PEGGY. That's okay.

BILLY. Hey. If Sean had made a pass, what would you have done?

PEGGY. God, I don't know. Gone confession-happy like Mom, I suppose.

BILLY. Still got a soft spot for him?

PEGGY. Maybe a little one.

BILLY. That's all?

PEGGY. Yeah.

BILLY. Well, too bad for him. You know, there's a rumor going around that he's thinking of giving up the collar. Maybe the two of you could work out something after all.

PEGGY. No. That's all I'd need. A man on the rebound from God.

BILLY. (*Moving to leave.*) Yeah, I guess so. Listen, I'm going to take myself to a movie.

PEGGY. (*Jumps.*) No, don't go. Stick around and keep me company. It's been a long time since we had a nice talk like this.

BILLY. I'm sorry. Let's both catch a movie. My treat.

PEGGY. Do you expect me to believe that you have the price of two movie theatre tickets in your pocket?

BILLY. Actually, I'm not even sure I have the price of one. I had to put gas in the car to get over here.

PEGGY. Why don't you just stay here? I don't want to

leave Mom alone anyway. She wasn't feeling very well earlier.

BILLY. What's the matter?

PEGGY. I'm not sure. She's asleep right now. She told me to wake her up in time for the late news. If she's not better by then, I'm going to give the doctor a call at home.

BILLY. That's a good idea. Hey, wanna play Scrabble?

PEGGY. Sure.

BILLY. Where's the set? Upstairs?

PEGGY. Yeah. In the hall closet.

BILLY. Great. (*He starts upstairs, exiting.*)

PEGGY. I'll make some popcorn.

BILLY. Now, you're talking! (*He exits upstairs, Peggy bolts to the phone and dials.*)

PEGGY. C'mon, Sean. Please pick up the phone.

BILLY. (*Offstage.*) Peg, I can't find it! Where else could it be?

PEGGY. Try my closet! And don't shout! Mom's trying to sleep! C'mon, Sean. Please. (*A look of dismay comes over her, and she puts on a fake voice.*) Good evening, Monsignor Ryan ... uh ... Would you be interested in some free dancing lessons? Yes, Sir ... Yes, I'm Catholic ... Yes, Sir ... Three Hail Mary's and a good Act of Contrition ... Yes, Monsignor ... Yes, Sir ... I'll start looking for a new job first thing tomorrow morning ... Good night. (*She hangs up, composes herself.*) To deadbolt the basement door, or not to deadbolt the basement door. That is the question. Oh, Sean, I hope you have more sense than I do. (*She exits toward the kitchen. Blackout.*)

ACT II, Scene 3

(*SETTING: The parish office.*

AT RISE: It is still Friday night. Sean is seated. Msgr. Ryan is pacing about, agitated.)

MSGR. RYAN. Sean, have you lost your senses?

SEAN. I have not lost my senses.

MSGR. RYAN. How could you have let something like this happen after I expressly told you to be careful?

SEAN. Don't I get any points for coming to you about it?

MSGR. RYAN. No. No, you don't. What you oughta get is the toe of my shoe up your cassock for doing exactly what I warned you not to do! Now, give me that key.

SEAN. I can't do that.

MSGR. RYAN. And why not?

SEAN. (*Grasping.*) Because getting rid of the key isn't going to make the door go away.

MSGR. RYAN. Huh?

SEAN. And ... I'm not entirely sure I want the door to go away.

MSGR. RYAN. Not entirely sure? Hey, Sean. You're supposed to be here to reaffirm your vocation. Not to diddle my parishioners!

SEAN. I'll thank you not to refer to it in those terms. It's much more than that.

MSGR. RYAN. You're right. It is much more than that. Sean, you don't seem to realize that the entire course of your life is on the line here.

SEAN. If you think I don't realize that, then you're the one who's lost his senses.

MSGR. RYAN. Didn't anything I said to you about what happened to me sink in?

SEAN. This is nothing like what happened to you.

MSGR. RYAN. Isn't it? Sean, whether you use that key tonight or not, this thing with Peggy is going to make your life a living hell. Answer me this: do you think you can really bring yourself to renounce your vows and leave the priesthood? To face all that a move like that would mean? Not to mention leaving a lifestyle that you've probably gotten pretty used to. There are more frightening things than celibacy in the life of a layman, my young friend.

SEAN. I don't know. Not yet, anyway. But I'm sure I'm capable of handling the decision.

MSGR. RYAN. Well, take it from me Father Connally. Handle this decision wrong, and you stand the chance of having it eat away at you for the rest of your life.

SEAN. You didn't handle your decision particularly smoothly, and you seem to have done all right. You made your peace. Why can't you leave me alone to make mine? Whichever way I have to go to do it?

MSGR. RYAN. Because I'm trying to spare you from a little heartache here! (*He composes himself.*) I didn't make my peace until well after I was ordained. Katy and Dan had a pretty long engagement. When they decided to give up on waiting 'til they could afford a place of their own, Katy called me to ask if I'd do the wedding. Like a fool I said "yes". I wanted to smack her for asking me. I think Dan did, too. But, what a girl wants at her wedding, a girl gets at her wedding ... As I heard their vows, the same rage I felt the day I had that fight with Dan came back at me like gangbusters. Pronouncing them man and wife left such a bitter taste in my mouth, I felt sick to my stomach. Then the organist kicked in and snapped me out of it. Then, as I watched them walk back down the aisle, all that anger turned into a guilt that made me feel even sicker. To this day, I beg God's forgiveness for the way I tainted the moment of that union ... and for the insult my feelings paid Him that day.

SEAN. Monsignor. I promise you. This is nothing like that.

MSGR. RYAN. Sean. If you go to her ... and raise her hopes, only to knock 'em down again, while at the same time giving the back of your hand to the Savior you've sworn to serve ... You'll have a very, very long way to go to make that peace.

SEAN. With all due respect, Monsignor, my life is not your life.

MSGR. RYAN. (*Exploding.*) Don't tell me about life! You overgrown boy! Life is not just your personal span of years and whims. Life is a force that will crush you like a cigarette in the gutter as soon as look at you! You'll live and die a thousand times before you go to God, Son. Just be sure to choose your deaths carefully. (*He moves to leave, calms down, turns back.*) Sean. Don't be a dope. All right?

SEAN. All right. (*Msgr. Ryan exits, upset with Sean and with himself, Sean remains alone for a moment, the telephone rings.*)

MRS. HARRIGAN. (*Offstage.*) I'll get it! (*Beat.*) Oh, dear! (*She enters.*) Father Connally! Sean, pick up the extension. It's Billy Thompson. His mother had another attack. Much worse than the others.

SEAN. Just tell him I'm on my way. (*He grabs a prayer book and sacramental oil from a shelf then exits.*)

MRS. HARRIGAN. (*On the phone.*) Billy? Billy, Father Connally says to tell you he's on his way. That's right. He just ran out the door. You get back to your mother. I'll say a prayer for her. (*She hangs up, pauses, exits shouting.*) Monsignor Ryan! Monsignor Ryan! (*Blackout.*)

(*SETTING: The Thompson living room.*

(*AT RISE: It is still Friday night. Mrs. Thompson lies on the sofa with a blanket over her. She is in something of a semi-conscious dream state. Peggy is kneeling beside her. Billy is on the phone.*)

BILLY. Hello ... Hello? Yes ... Please, don't put me on hold again ... Thanks ... This is Bill Thompson ... I called about twenty minutes ago ... Good evening to you, too; where the hell is my mother's ambulance! What? ... Where is it coming from, the Mayo Clinic? ... All right, all right ... Yes, I understand ... uh, huh ... Right ... Oh, don't worry, we're not going anywhere ... Thanks. (*He hangs up.*)

PEGGY. What's going on?

BILLY. Some idiot downtown decided to torch his factory during the nightshift and tie up every ambulance in town. Even if they had one available it probably couldn't get past the fire trucks without taking the long way around.

PEGGY. That means the doctor will be forever getting here, too. His service said he was down at hospital. That's it. Help me get her into the car.

BILLY. Peg, they said not to move her. That could be worse than making her wait.

PEGGY. We have to do something!

BILLY. Peggy, calm down. There's nothing we can do except keep her comfortable and wait. (*Sean runs on from the kitchen entrance, Billy is visibly startled.*)

PEGGY. (*Throws her arms around Sean.*) Sean!

SEAN. How is she?

PEGGY. She'll be better now. She was calling for you before.

BILLY. Peg, she's been calling for Dad, too. Please, don't get your hopes up about this.

SEAN. Is there an ambulance on the way?

PEGGY. There's a fire or something holding them up. Sean, please. Do something for her.

SEAN. Okay, okay. Easy, now. Billy, take your sister into the kitchen and make her a cup of tea.

PEGGY. I don't want any tea.

BILLY. C'mon, sister. I'll prove to you that I can boil water. (*They exit toward kitchen. Beat. Sean kneels beside Mrs. Thompson, anoints her and prays silently. Msgr. Ryan bolts in through the front door.*)

SEAN. Hello.

MSGR. RYAN. Hello, Sean. The front door was open so I just ... I guess they wanted to get as much air into the room as they could.

SEAN. Probably.

MSGR. RYAN. Where are they?

SEAN. In the kitchen. Peggy was pretty shook up, so I told Billy to make her some tea.

MSGR. RYAN. Plain tea?

SEAN. Yeah.

MSGR. RYAN. You are young and stupid, aren't you? Ordinary tea is for ordinary circumstances. (*He looks around the room, spots a bottle of whiskey, picks it up and hands it to Sean.*) Here. And give it a proper spiking. Don't use a shot glass or I'll tell your old man on you. I'll stay with Mrs. Thompson.

SEAN. (*Exiting toward kitchen.*) Yes, Sir. (*Msgr. Ryan turns slowly toward Mrs. Thompson.*)

MSGR. RYAN. Aw, Katy. Katy, Katy Gallagher.

MRS. THOMPSON. Dan? Dan? Is that you?

MSGR. RYAN. (*At a loss.*) I, uh ...

MRS. THOMPSON. I know I've aged, Dan. But surely I'm not unrecognizable.

MSGR. RYAN. (*Affecting a voice.*) Um. Well, jeez, Babe. Sure I recognize ya. It's just that you look so young. You had me speechless for a minute.

MRS. THOMPSON. Save that for your girlfriends, Thompson. How did you get here?

MSGR. RYAN. Huh? Oh, I'm on a Purgatory furlough. Good behavior. All those candles you've been spending my social security on must be kicking in, too.

MRS. THOMPSON. Oh, I'm glad for you, Dan. But I'm sad, too. Even if I'm lucky enough to get into Purgatory, you'll be out way before me. Will you wait for me, Dan?

MSGR. RYAN. Wait for you? I'm not gonna have to wait for you. That's the other reason I came to see you. I've got a message for you from the top. The Big Guy says there's not gonna be even a minute of Purgatory for you. He says that any woman with moxie enough to stand being married to me deserves an express trip to the Pearly Gates. He says I don't deserve you. And He's right, of course. But Katy ... You've gotta know that I always loved you. If I'd known any better, I'd have done better by you. I swear. (*Sean returns, realizes what's happening, enters the room quietly.*)

MRS. THOMPSON. Don't be swearing, Dan. He'll hear us and then we'll have to get Father Sean to come over for Confession. And I don't think priests are allowed to hear confessions from dead people. (*Msgr. Ryan spots Sean.*)

MSGR. RYAN. That's another thing. God says you're to stop confessing all the time unless you can come up with something He hasn't heard before. He says you're starting to sound like a broken record. And that you're to stop driving that fine young priest up the wall with your worrying.

MRS. THOMPSON. Is He very mad at me, Dan?

MSGR. RYAN. No, Babe. It's not that He's mad. It's just that He doesn't like to see you worrying for no good reason.

MRS. THOMPSON. Well, if I really have no reason to worry, it's only because God sent me Father Sean. If he wasn't so good at his job, who knows where I might have ended up?

MSGR. RYAN. Yeah, you big sinner. Say a prayer for him.

MRS. THOMPSON. I will. Besides, I think I owe him for insulting him.

MSGR. RYAN. What do you mean, Babe?

MRS. THOMPSON. I have a feeling that Father Sean is

really that hairy Connally boy Peggy went with in high school. I was looking at their prom picture the other day and there sure seems to be a strong resemblance between the two of them. I'm afraid I said some nasty things about the way he used to be when I didn't know who he used to be.

MSGR. RYAN. Don't lose any sleep over it. He probably had it coming.

MRS. THOMPSON. Who would have thought that terror would make a priest? And such a good one, too?

MSGR. RYAN. Yeah. Who'd have thunk it?

MRS. THOMPSON. Dan. You don't think my insulting a priest will change God's mind about Purgatory, do you?

MSGR. RYAN. Katy, if I hear you accuse yourself of one more thing, so help me, I'll belt ya! I've got divine permission.

MRS. THOMPSON. Yes, Sir. Dan ... What about Francis Ryan? (*Beat.*)

MSGR. RYAN. What about him?

MRS. THOMPSON. Oh God. I need Father Sean. I never even told him about Francis. Where is he, Dan? I heard Peggy say that he was coming over before.

SEAN. (*Going to her.*) Mrs. Thompson. Mrs. Thompson, did I just hear you call for me?

MRS. THOMPSON. Father Sean. Oh, thank God you're here. I've got to ask you something about Francis Ryan. Monsignor Ryan.

SEAN. Sure. Go ahead.

MRS. THOMPSON. You see ... He and I were friends of a sort at one time. But Dan and I were better friends. And Francis was going to be a priest anyway. But Francis got so mad when Dan and I got engaged. I'm afraid I might have driven him into the priesthood and deprived him of a family and ... Oh, Father, do you think I did wrong by him? And do you think I can be forgiven for it? I mean, God's been so nice. Letting Dan out on furlough and all. Can you see Dan, Father?

SEAN. No. No, Mrs. Thompson. I can't.

MRS. THOMPSON. I didn't think you'd be able to. Father

... What about Francis?

SEAN. Let me tell you something, Mrs. Thompson. Nobody drove Francis Ryan, or Sean Connally, into the priesthood. We were called to it. So don't give it another thought.

MRS. THOMPSON. Thank you, Father. Thank you ever so much. Dan?

MSGR. RYAN. Yeah, Babe?

MRS. THOMPSON. Can't you even hear him, Father Sean?

SEAN. I'm afraid not, Mrs. Thompson.

MRS. THOMPSON. Dan, did you hear? Everything's all right. Oh, but if you're only out on furlough, what if I should die before you get out for good? Are you allowed visitors?

MSGR. RYAN. There's talk of an early parole. They said they might consider releasing me into your custody.

MRS. THOMPSON. For keeps?

MSGR. RYAN. For keeps, Babe. Just you and me.

MRS. THOMPSON. Oh, Dan. I've been wishing for that since the day you died.

MSGR. RYAN. Careful what you wish for, Katy. You just might get it.

MRS. THOMPSON. That's what my father said to my mother when she wished I'd get married and I brought you home.

MSGR. RYAN. Well, bad cess to them. Now stop yammerin' and get some rest, girl.

MRS. THOMPSON. Okay, Dan. Will I see you again soon?

MSGR. RYAN. Sure thing, Babe. Real soon. (*He kisses her on the forehead.*) G'night, Katy.

MRS. THOMPSON. Good night, Dan.

(*Mrs. Thompson passes out. Msgr. Ryan and Sean exchange anxious glances. Sean kneels beside Mrs. Thompson and begins reading the prayers for the dying aloud from a prayer book. Msgr. Ryan exits slowly as Sean reads. Fade lights to black.*)

(*When the lights return, Sean is alone in the room.*

Billy enters through the front door.)

BILLY. The ambulance just pulled away.

SEAN. What did the paramedics say?

BILLY. There wasn't much they could say. She's got no vital signs.

SEAN. Did your sister go with her?

BILLY. Yeah. She followed in my car. Care for a nip at the altar wine, Father?

SEAN. Why not? I don't think the Monsignor will catch us in the sacristy at this hour.

BILLY. Not unless he comes in for a belt himself. (*He checks the liquor supply.*) Nothing left but this sweet stuff Mom likes. I blew the last of the Irish spiking my sister's tea. Maybe there's some beer in the fridge.

SEAN. Sounds good. (*Billy goes to the kitchen. Sean takes the infamous key from his pocket, contemplates it a moment, then tosses it on the floor. Billy returns.*)

BILLY. (*Handing Sean a beer.*) Make it count, Reverend. These are the last two in the fridge.

SEAN. Hey, Billy. Did you drop a key? There's one on the floor over there.

BILLY. Nice try, Sean. Think I didn't notice that you came in through the kitchen before?

SEAN. Yeah, well, I was in a hurry. The basement door is closer to the rectory.

BILLY. You can leave it there if you want. But you'd still have to face up to Peg. If you didn't, I'd have to kick the hell out of you. Nothing personal or anything. I've just got this rule that nobody is allowed to upset her but me. It's a rule she doesn't know about, by the way.

SEAN. She won't hear about it from me. (*A lull.*) Hey. Did you ever really steal a swig of altar wine?

BILLY. Yeah. Once.

SEAN. Nasty stuff this parish buys, isn't it?

BILLY. God, it was awful. I'm surprised it didn't put me off drinking for life. It was on Christmas Eve. Just before Midnight Mass. Me, Bobby Maguire, and Brian Ahearn managed to swipe a bottle from the sacristy and sneak it out to the alleyway between the church and the rectory.

SEAN. What kind of shape were you in for Mass?

BILLY. The worst. There the three of us are. Standing out in the snow in our shirtsleeves. Passing around this bottle and pretending the stuff doesn't taste like battery acid. And it had been a long time since dinner. So the stuff was hitting us like a ton of bricks. And that was outside in the cold. Can you imagine what it was like inside? With those heating pipes underneath the pews?

SEAN. And the air thick with incense.

BILLY. Oh, God. Anyway, we start the procession, see? And I'm holding onto Bobby Maguire's surplice so's not to wander out of line. And all he has to steady himself on is Brian Ahearn. All the way around the church I'm wondering, "What's the penalty for throwing up at Midnight Mass?"

SEAN. They got pretty lenient on that after Vatican Two.

BILLY. Well, fortunately I didn't have to find out. That was my one piece of luck. Just as our part of the procession is passing where my family is sitting, I let go of Bobby Maguire's surplice, so my old man doesn't see me holding on. And —

SEAN. Oh, no.

BILLY. Right into my father's lap. Ooh, the look in that man's eyes.

SEAN. What did he do?

BILLY. Let's just say that he was none to happy about having to leave Mass early. Especially with a queasy altar boy over his shoulder.

SEAN. And he let you live?

BILLY. I survived. Only through the intercession of St. Mom. She was always good like that. About me getting into trouble and all. (*His mother's absence starts to get the better of him.*) Sean. I need to get out of here for awhile. Peg told me to stay by the phone. Would you listen out for it? I won't be gone long.

SEAN. No problem. Where are you going? In case she

calls.

BILLY. I don't know. Light a candle maybe.

SEAN. I doubt she needs it.

BILLY. It's not for her. I just can't shake this picture of my mom sitting on a cloud waiting for my father. And waiting, and waiting, and waiting. God, I loved him. But I'm afraid the poor guy did go out with a few strikes against him. I won't be gone long.

SEAN. (*Tossing Billy a set of keys.*) Take your time. Here. Take these. The church'll be locked up at this hour. The round one is the key to the sacristy door.

BILLY. First church key I ever saw that actually works on a church.

SEAN. Yeah, well just stay away from the altar wine.

BILLY. Okay. Sean, about that crack I made about my rule —

SEAN. Hey, c'mon. Don't be a dope. All right?

BILLY. Yeah.

SEAN. Now get going. I'll see you later.

BILLY. Thanks, Sean. (*Peggy returns, running into Billy.*)

BILLY. Whoa, Peg! What's the matter?

PEGGY. Nothing. I just realized I didn't have Mom's insurance card with me. Everything else in this world costs money. Dying isn't any different. Where are you off to?

BILLY. I, uh, I blew the last of the Irish on that tea you wasted before. I was just going down to the late-night for more so's I could pour the padre one for the road. He was going to listen out for the phone for me.

PEGGY. Do me a favor before you go? Just run upstairs and get that card for me. It should be in her top bureau drawer. I just don't think I could handle being in her room alone right now.

BILLY. Sure, Peg. (*Billy exits. Peggy and Sean are left alone to face each other.*)

SEAN. Are you okay?

PEGGY. For now. If I go up there I won't be. So ... Any news on when you're going back to St. Michael's?

SEAN. Well, the deal was for a month. So, I guess it'll be next week. Back to the backwoods, as the Monsignor says.

PEGGY. What are you going to do with your last weekend in the big city?

SEAN. Spend it with my father, if I know what's good for me. He says I ignore him.

PEGGY. Blame it on us. We've kept you pretty busy.

SEAN. He'll get over it. I'll let him beat me at darts. Is Billy going to stay with you tonight?

PEGGY. No. He'd never make it back out to school in time tomorrow. What with the traffic and all going out that way in the morning. He'll go out there tonight, get somebody to cover for him at work, get somebody to take notes for him. That sort of thing.

SEAN. Then he's coming back?

PEGGY. Yeah. He's going to stay at home 'til after the funeral. Says he won't hear of me being by myself.

SEAN. You're going to spend your first night without her all alone?

PEGGY. I don't know. (*A few beats as the unspoken question hangs in the air.*)

SEAN. Peg, I — I guess I never really seriously intended to quit. I'm either a hopelessly dedicated priest, or an incredible coward.

PEGGY. I think it's the first one. I heard it in your voice when you were praying over Mom.

SEAN. I did feel like I belonged there with her.

PEGGY. Did you absolutely have to come back here? Couldn't you have just wandered in the desert for forty days and forty nights, or something?

SEAN. It had to be here, Peg. I learned a few things around here that I just plain forgot along the way.

PEGGY. Can I ask? Or is it one of those priest things that women aren't supposed to be able to understand?

SEAN. (*After pausing to think.*) I'd forgotten that I'm necessary. Even if that just means being there. Sooner or later, we all need someone who looks like us, and sounds like us, to stand between us and that other life we're promised. To assure us that it's there, and that we've got a real chance at it. No matter how ordinary our lives are. That's what I always admired about guys like Monsignor Ryan. They can look at the incredible simplicity of everyday life and find a worthy path to God in it. Standing there, between your mother and eternity ... Assuring her that she'd be welcome on the other side ... I remembered why it's important for me to do this job. (*Beat.*) And to do it without distractions. (*He watches that thought drift in the air a moment.*) I'm sorry, Peg.

PEGGY. For what? For keeping us both out of trouble?

SEAN. For dragging you into my problem.

PEGGY. No. It was our problem. I knew I had things to deal with the second I heard you were coming over here that first day.

SEAN. And?

PEGGY. And, when all is said and done, I guess I'm not all that unhappy about your decision.

SEAN. I'm not even going to be allowed to leave here feeling flattered, am I?

PEGGY. You know that's not what I mean. (*Beat.*)

SEAN. (*Picking up "the key".*) Peg, did you lose a key. There's one laying here.

PEGGY. You know, I was just looking for that this afternoon.

SEAN. Well, it's easy to miss. With that big, stupid I "heart" you keychain. (*They share a resolved smile as Billy returns, carrying a sheaf of papers.*)

BILLY. Peg, I tore the room apart twice, but I couldn't find it. There's a bunch of papers about the policy, but no card.

PEGGY. (*Taking the papers.*) It's probably stuffed into the pocket of a housedress somewhere. I'll just take the whole mess down there. At least I've got the policy number. Let them figure out the rest. (*She turns toward Sean.*) See ya in church. (*She exits.*)

BILLY. Sean, after being in that room, I really have to get out of here. Will you call Dr. McCabe at the hospital and tell him she's running behind?

SEAN. Sure. No problem.

BILLY. Thanks. See ya later. (*He exits. Sean goes to the telephone and dials information.*)

SEAN. Hello. Can I have the number for the emergency room at Mercy General, please ... Thank you. (*He dials again.*) Hello? Mercy General Emergency? This is Father Connally from Contrition parish. Will you page Dr. McCabe for me, please? Thank you. (*While waiting his attention is caught by an index card laying nearby. He picks it up and reads aloud from it.*) 'I acknowledged my sin to you. My guilt I covered not. I said, 'I confess my faults to the Lord' ... and you took away the guilt of my sin.' Maybe I'd better hang on to this. (*He pockets the card, and begins whistling to pass the time on hold. His father, Joseph Connally, pokes his head through the front door.*)

CONNALLY. Pssst. Are you alone? (*Sean waves him in. Connally ducks outside and returns pushing a dolly. On the dolly is a beer keg. Sitting on the beer keg is Tipples Nolan, asleep.*) I saw a car with siren lights pulling away. I thought she called the cops on you or something.

SEAN. That was an ambulance. And I'm taking you to the eye doctor. (*His attention turns toward the phone.*) Hello. Dr. McCabe? This is Father Connally ... That's right, Sean Connally ... I'm just calling to let you know that Peggy Keenan is running a few minutes late. She turned back to pick up some insurance forms she might need ... Okay ... Goodbye. (*He hangs up, then turns to survey the sight of Connally and Tipples.*) So, what are the two of you doing haunting the streets at this time of night?

CONNALLY. Connally's car service, at your service. With a fleet of one. Mrs. Tipples told me over the phone, in no uncertain terms, that she has no intention of coming out to claim her champion. Wounded though he is. So, I'm giving the old boy a lift home.

SEAN. Couldn't you just call him a cab?

CONNALLY. I'm afraid of what he might do to the inside of a cab. I suppose that was Katy they were taking away.

SEAN. Yeah.

CONNALLY. What are her chances?

SEAN. She was gone before they even got here.

CONNALLY. (*Making the sign of the cross.*) God be good to her. And how about you? Have you got yourself straightened out? Or should I plan on moving where nobody knows me?

SEAN. Don't worry. What's left of the family honor is still intact.

CONNALLY. Well, thank God for that. You ought to be ashamed of yourself. Messing around with that poor lonely girl's life.

SEAN. I know.

CONNALLY. It's all right for you. You have the Church to look out for you. To make a life for you. What does she have? Nothing but that airhead brother of hers. (*Beat.*) Say. I wonder if Peggy's ever been to Atlantic City. (*Sean walks threateningly toward Connally. Blackout.*)

• • •

FIRST NIGHT

Romantic Comedy. Jack Neary. 1m. 1f. Int. A bright, warm, witty comedy about dreams, life, and love that had critics and audiences cheering from coast to coast. On a sorely uneventful New Year's Eve, Danny Fleming is waiting to close up the video store where he works. But on this night, Meredith O'Connor walks in. She and Danny were an adolescent item back in parochial school, back before she became a nun. Now, as she has re-enters the secular world, she hopes to pick things up where they left off. It is a first night to remember as Danny realizes dreams aren't just something to hold at arm's length. "Considerable charm, zest, imagination, and expertise ..." — *Variety.* "Sweet, fast, funny ... a lovely riff of magic." — *Boston Globe.* "A crisp and neatly starched little heart-warmer." — *Newsday.*

NEW PLAYS 1995

ALICE IN LOVE
AN EVENING OF CULTURE: (FAITH
COUNTY II)
ASHES TO ASHES, CRUST TO CRUST
CINDERELLA: IT'S OKAY TO BE
DIFFERENT
FACE 2 FACE
HIDE AND SHRIEK
MY MOM'S DAD
ONCE UPON A BEGINNING
QUEEN FOR A DAY
REMOVING THE GLOVE
REUNION
STIFF CUFFS
THE EXPLORATORS CLUB
THIRTEEN PAST MIDNIGHT
VOICES 2,000
WINNING MONOLOGUES FROM THE
BEGINNINGS WORKSHOP

Write for information regarding availability

Baker's Plays
100 Chauncy Street
Boston, MA 02111

NEW PLAYS 1996

BEAUTIFUL GIRLS AND OTHER
WINNING PLAYS
BUTLER DID IT, AGAIN!
DICKENS' CHRISTMAS CAROL
GIRLS TO THE RESCUE
GRAND CHRISTMAS HISTORY OF THE
ANDY LANDY CLAN
LITTLE MATCH GIRL
PRINCESS PLAYS
SANDBAG STAGE LEFT
SGANARELLE
SNAPSHOTS
SNOWBALL AND OTHER PLAYS
TRIPLE DATE
TURN AROUND

Write for information regarding availability

Baker's Plays
100 Chauncy Street
Boston, MA 02111

NEW PLAYS 1997

ACTS & CONTRITION
ALL THE WORLD'S A STAGE
THE AMERICAN CAR
THE BROADWAY CAFE
BEAUTY AND THE BEAST
THE DULLSVILLE MYSTERY
THE EIGHT: REINDEER MONOLOGUES
THE FIANCÉ
AN IMPECCABLE LARCENY
A MIDSUMMER NIGHT'S DREAM
MUCH ADO ABOUT NOTHING
ONCE UPON A WOLF
PERCHANCE TO DREAM
THE PHONY PHYSICIAN
RADIO T.B.S.
RED LETTER DAY
RUTHERFORD WOLF
THE SECRET GARDEN
SOMETHING DIFFERENT
SOUTHERN FRIED MURDER
TV OR NOT TV
UBU PLAYS
WAITING FOR CAPTAIN HA HA

Write for information regarding availability

Baker's Plays
100 Chauncy Street
Boston, MA 02111